MW00899117

The Ultimate
GLUTEN-FREE
HOLIDAY COOKBOOK

Celebrate the Season with Delicious Gluten-Free Cakes, Breads, and Desserts for Every Occasion

Samantha Reed

INTRODUCTION

Welcome to The Ultimate Gluten-Free Holiday Cookbook! This collection of recipes is your invitation to celebrate the magic of the holidays while enjoying delicious gluten-free treats that bring warmth, joy, and flavor to every special moment. Whether it's the cozy gatherings of Christmas, the fresh blooms of Easter, or family feasts throughout the year, this book has been crafted with care to ensure everyone can enjoy the sweet, savory, and festive flavors that make these occasions unforgettable.

Each recipe in this book has been thoughtfully developed to capture the essence of traditional holiday baking, reimagined without gluten but with all the taste, texture, and pleasure intact. For many, the holidays wouldn't be complete without gingerbread houses, fruitcakes infused with a hint of brandy, or fresh-baked bread filling the kitchen with its comforting aroma. Now, with a few simple ingredients and techniques, you can recreate these beloved classics in gluten-free form, bringing festive flavors to the table that everyone can savor.

Throughout these pages, you'll find everything from hearty breads and savory rolls to rich cakes, pies, and cookies—all crafted to be enjoyed as you celebrate with loved ones. You'll discover familiar favorites, new festive ideas, and tips for perfecting gluten-free baking, from ingredient substitutions to baking techniques that ensure every treat is as delicious and beautiful as you remember.

Whether you're baking for family, friends, or even a special occasion at work, The Ultimate Gluten-Free Holiday Cookbook will inspire you to create and share delightful treats that make any holiday memorable. So preheat your oven, gather your ingredients, and let's bake our way through the year's most wonderful celebrations, gluten-free style!

Here's to creating delicious memories, one gluten-free holiday treat at a time.

Contents

BREADS

Rustic Artisan Loaf

Nutrition

Calories: 150 | Protein: 3g | Carbohydrate: 28g | Fat: 4g |
Fiber: 2g

Ingredients

3 cups all-purpose flour (gluten-free
blend)
1 teaspoon xanthan gum (if not
included in the flour blend)
1 packet (2 ¼ teaspoons) active dry
yeast (gluten-free)
1 ½ cups warm water
1 tablespoon sugar
1 teaspoon salt
2 tablespoons olive oil
1 tablespoon apple cider vinegar
Extra flour (gluten-free) for dusting

Instructions

1. Take a small shallow bowl and mix the warm water, sugar,
   and yeast. Put it aside for 5-10 minutes until frothy and bubbly.
2. In a large, deep-bottom bowl, combine the flour, xanthan gum (if
   using), and salt.
3. Add tow tbsp oil and apple cider vinegar to the yeast mixture,
   then slowly pour the wet ingredients into the dry mixture. Stir
   properly with a wooden spoon until the dough forms.
4. Cover the dough with the clean kitchen towel or plastic wrap.
   Put it aside to rise in a warm place for 1-1.5 hours.
5. Lightly dust the surface with flour. Shape the dough and put it on
   a parchment paper-arranged baking sheet. Cover and put it aside
   to rise for another 34-45 minutes.
6. Preheat oven to 425°F (220°C). Place a cast-iron skillet or baking
   dish with water on the bottom rack of the oven. Score the top of
   the loaf with 2-3 slashes using a sharp knife.
7. Bake the loaf for 30-35 minutes until the crust turns golden
   brown. Cool on the wire rack for 18-20 minutes.

Prep Time:
15 mins

Cook Time:
35 mins

Serving
10 slices

Classic Sourdough Bread

Nutrition

Calories: 160 | Protein: 4g | Carbohydrate: 30g | Fat: 2g |
Fiber: 3g

Ingredients

3 cups gluten-free sourdough
starter
4 cups gluten-free all-purpose flour
1 teaspoon xanthan gum (if not in
flour mix)
1 ½ teaspoons salt
1 ½ cups warm water
1 tablespoon olive oil

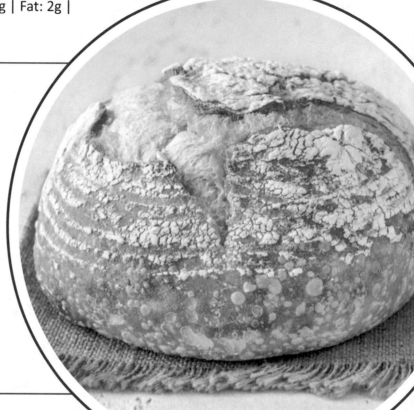

Instructions

1. Mix the sourdough starter and warm water in a large bowl.
   Stir until combined.
2. Add gluten-free flour, xanthan gum (if needed), and salt. Mix
   until the dough forms.
3. Knead the dough for 4-5 minutes, place cloth to cover it, and let
   it ferment at room temperature for 12-24 hours.
4. After fermentation, turn the dough onto a floured surface and
   shape it into a loaf.
5. Let the loaf rise for 1-2 hours until it has puffed slightly.
6. Preheat oven to 450°F (230°C). Put the Dutch oven inside
   it. Place the dough in the Dutch pan, cover, and bake for 30
   minutes.
7. Remove the lid and bake more for 5-10 minutes until golden
   brown. Cool before slicing.

**Prep Time:
20 mins**

**Cook Time:
35 mins**

**Serving
12 slices**

Herb-Infused Focaccia

Nutrition

Calories: 180 | Protein: 3g | Carbohydrate: 32g | Fat: 6g |
Fiber: 2g

Ingredients

3 cups gluten-free all-purpose flour
1 teaspoon xanthan gum (if not in
flour mix)
2 teaspoons active dry yeast
1 ½ cups warm water
2 tablespoons olive oil
1 teaspoon salt
1 tablespoon fresh rosemary,
chopped
1 tablespoon fresh thyme, chopped
1 teaspoon garlic powder

Instructions

1. Take a small shallow bowl and mix warm water, yeast, and
   one tbsp oil. Let sit for 5-10 minutes until frothy.
2. Take a deep-bottom bowl and combine gluten-free flour, xanthan
   gum (if using), salt, and garlic powder.
3. Slowly add yeast mixture to the dry elements, mixing until a
   dough forms. Toss in chopped herbs.
4. Cover the dough and put it aside for 1.5 hours in a warm area.
5. Preheat oven to 400°F (200°C). Press the dough toward the
   greased baking pan bottom, creating dimples with your fingers.
6. Drizzle leftover olive oil and sprinkle with extra rosemary and
   thyme.
7. Bake for 20-25 minutes until golden. Cool before slicing.

**Prep Time:
20 mins**

**Cook Time:
25 mins**

**Serving
10 slices**

Hearty Multigrain Bread

Nutrition

Calories: 200 | Protein: 5g | Carbohydrate: 32g | Fat: 6g | Fiber: 5g

Ingredients

2 cups gluten-free all-purpose flour
1 cup gluten-free oat flour
½ cup flaxseed meal
¼ cup sunflower seeds
1 tablespoon chia seeds
1 packet (2 ¼ teaspoons) active dry yeast
1 ½ cups warm water
1 tablespoon honey
1 teaspoon salt
1 tablespoon olive oil

Instructions

1. Mix warm water with honey, and yeast in a small dee-bottom bowl. Let sit for 5-10 minutes until bubbly.
2. Take a deep-bottom bowl and combine all-purpose flour, oat flour, flaxseed meal, sunflower seeds, chia seeds, and salt.
3. Add yeast mixture and one tbsp oil to the dry elements and mix until a dough forms.
4. Knead for a few minutes, cover and let rise for one hour in a warm area.
5. Preheat oven to 375°F (190°C). Shape the dough into a loaf and place in a greased loaf pan.
6. Bake for 37-40 minutes until the loaf sounds when tapped.
7. Let the bread cool completely before slicing.

**Prep Time:
20 mins**

**Cook Time:
40 mins**

**Serving
12 slices**

Everyday Sandwich Bread

Nutrition

Calories: 160 | Protein: 3g | Carbohydrate: 30g | Fat: 4g |
Fiber: 2g

Ingredients

3 cups gluten-free all-purpose flour
1 teaspoon xanthan gum (if not in
flour mix)
2 teaspoons active dry yeast
1 ½ cups warm water
1 tablespoon honey
1 tablespoon olive oil
1 teaspoon salt

Instructions

1. Take a small shallow bowl and mix warm water, honey, and
    yeast. Let sit for 5-10 minutes until frothy.
2. Take a deep-bottom bowl and combine the flour, xanthan gum (if
    needed), and salt.
3. Slowly pour the yeast mixture and one tbsp oil into the dry
    ingredients, stirring until a dough forms.
4. Knead the dough for a few minutes, put its cover, and put it aside
    for 1 hour in a warm area.
5. Preheat oven to 375°F (190°C). Shape the dough into a loaf and
    place in a greased loaf pan.
6. Bake for 30-35 minutes until the loaf sounds hollow when
    tapped.
7. Leave it aside to cool before slicing.

Prep Time:
15 mins

Cook Time:
35 mins

Serving
12 slices

Italian Ciabatta Rolls

Nutrition

Calories: 180 | Protein: 4g | Carbohydrate: 32g | Fat: 4g |
Fiber: 2g

Ingredients

3 cups gluten-free all-purpose flour
1 teaspoon xanthan gum
1 ½ teaspoons active dry yeast
1 ½ cups warm water
1 teaspoon sugar
1 teaspoon salt
2 tablespoons olive oil

Instructions

1. Mix the warm water, sugar, and yeast in a bowl. Let sit for 5-10 minutes until frothy.
2. Take a deep-bottom bowl and combine flour, xanthan gum (if needed), and salt.
3. Slowly pour in the yeast mixture and two tbsp oil, stirring to form a sticky dough.
4. Knead for a few minutes, then put the cloth cover and leave for 1 hour until it doubles in size.
5. Preheat oven to 425°F (220°C). Arrange the baking sheet with parchment paper.
6. Shape the dough into 8 rolls and place them on the baking sheet.
7. Bake for 20-25 minutes until the top surface turns golden brown and crispy. Cool on a wire rack.

**Prep Time:
20 mins**

**Cook Time:
25 mins**

**Serving
8 rolls**

CRISPY FRENCH BAGUETTE

Nutrition

Calories: 130 | Protein: 3g | Carbohydrate: 26g | Fat: 2g | Fiber: 2g

Ingredients

3 cups gluten-free all-purpose flour
1 teaspoon xanthan gum
1 packet (2 ¼ teaspoons) active dry yeast
1 ½ cups warm water
1 teaspoon sugar
1 teaspoon salt
1 tablespoon olive oil

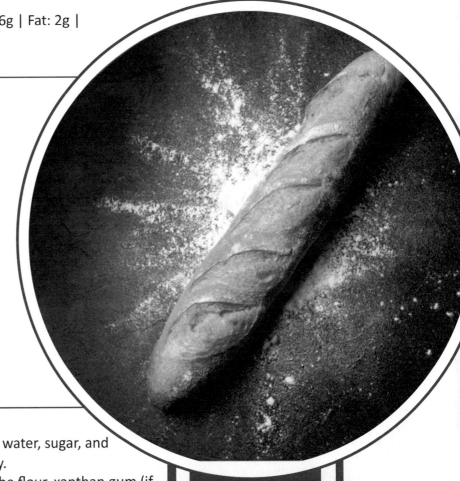

Instructions

1. Take a small shallow bowl and mix warm water, sugar, and yeast. Let sit for 5-10 minutes until frothy.
2. Take a deep-bottom bowl and combine the flour, xanthan gum (if using), and salt.
3. Add yeast mixture and olive oil, stirring to form a dough. Knead for 5 minutes.
4. Cover the dough and let rise for 1.5 hours in a warm, draft-free area.
5. Preheat oven to 450°F (230°C). Shape the dough into a long baguette and place it on a parchment paper-arranged baking sheet.
6. Score the top surface of the dough with a sharp knife. Bake for 25-30 minutes until golden brown.
7. Let the baguette cool before slicing.

**Prep Time:
20 mins**

**Cook Time:
30 mins**

**Serving
12 slices**

Sweet Honey Cornbread

Nutrition

Calories: 190 | Protein: 4g | Carbohydrate: 29g | Fat: 6g |
Fiber: 2g

Ingredients

1 cup gluten-free cornmeal
1 cup gluten-free all-purpose flour
1 teaspoon xanthan gum
1 tablespoon baking powder
½ teaspoon salt
1 cup milk (or dairy-free alternative)
¼ cup honey
¼ cup melted butter (or coconut oil)
2 large eggs

Instructions

1. Preheat oven to 400°F (200°C). Grease an 8-inch baking dish.
2. Grab the deep-bottom bowl and toss the cornmeal, flour, xanthan gum (if needed), baking powder, and salt.
3. In another deep-bottom bowl, whisk the milk, honey, melted butter, and eggs until combined.
4. Slowly add the wet elements mixture to the dry elements mixture, stirring until just combined.
5. Drop batter into the greased baking dish and smooth the top.
6. Bake for 20-25 minutes until golden brown and a toothpick comes out clean.
7. Cool for 10 minutes before, then slice into squares.

Prep Time:
10 mins

Cook Time:
25 mins

Serving
9 squares

Zucchini Walnut Bread

Nutrition

Calories: 210 | Protein: 4g | Carbohydrate: 28g | Fat: 10g |
Fiber: 3g

Ingredients

2 cups gluten-free all-purpose flour
1 teaspoon xanthan gum (if not in
flour mix)
1 teaspoon baking powder
½ teaspoon baking soda
1 teaspoon cinnamon
¼ teaspoon salt
2 large eggs
½ cup coconut sugar
½ cup melted coconut oil
1 teaspoon vanilla extract
1 ½ cups grated zucchini (excess
water squeezed out)
½ cup chopped walnuts

Instructions

1. Preheat oven to 350°F (175°C). Grease a 9x5-inch loaf pan.
2. Grab the medium shallow bowl and whisk the flour, xanthan gum
   (if using), baking powder, baking soda, cinnamon, and salt.
3. In another deep-bottom bowl, whisk the eggs, coconut sugar
   melted coconut oil, and vanilla extract.
4. Add dry elements mixture to the wet elements mixture, mixing
   until combined. Toss in the grated zucchini and chopped walnuts.
5. Ladle batter into the oil-greased pan and smooth the top. Bake
   for 47-50 minutes until a tooth-stick is inserted comes out clean.
6. Cool in the pan for 10 minutes.

**Prep Time:
15 mins**

**Cook Time:
50 mins**

**Serving
10 slices**

Moist Banana Bread

Nutrition

Calories: 220 | Protein: 4g | Carbohydrate: 30g | Fat: 9g | Fiber: 2g

Ingredients

2 cups gluten-free all-purpose flour
1 teaspoon xanthan gum
1 teaspoon baking soda
½ teaspoon baking powder
½ teaspoon cinnamon
¼ teaspoon salt
½ cup melted butter (or coconut oil)
¾ cup coconut sugar
2 large eggs
1 teaspoon vanilla extract
3 ripe bananas, mashed
½ cup chopped walnuts (optional)

Instructions

1. Preheat oven to 350°F (175°C). Grease a 9x5-inch loaf pan.
2. Grab the medium shallow bowl and toss the flour, xanthan gum, baking soda, baking powder, cinnamon, and salt.
3. Take a deep-bottom bowl and mix the melted butter and coconut sugar until well combined. Add eggs and vanilla extract, mixing well.
4. Toss in the mashed bananas until smooth. Slowly add dry elements mixture to the wet elements mixture and mix until combined. Fold in the walnuts if using.
5. Ladle batter into the oil-greased pan and smooth the top.
6. Bake for 50-55 minutes until a tooth-stick comes out clean.
7. Cool the banana bread for 10 minutes.

Prep Time: 15 mins

Cook Time: 55 mins

Serving 10 slices

Spiced Pumpkin Loaf

Nutrition

Calories: 190 | Protein: 3g | Carbohydrate: 28g | Fat: 8g |
Fiber: 2g

Ingredients

1 ¾ cups gluten-free all-purpose
flour
1 teaspoon xanthan gum (if not in
flour mix)
1 teaspoon baking soda
1 teaspoon baking powder
1 tablespoon pumpkin spice
½ teaspoon salt
1 cup pumpkin puree
½ cup coconut sugar
½ cup melted coconut oil
2 large eggs
1 teaspoon vanilla extract

Instructions

1. Preheat oven to 350°F (175°C). Grease a 9x5-inch loaf pan.
2. Grab the medium shallow bowl and toss the flour, xanthan gum,
    baking soda, baking powder, pumpkin spice, and salt.
3. Take a deep-bottom bowl and mix the pumpkin puree, coconut
    sugar, melted coconut oil with eggs, and vanilla extract until
    smooth.
4. Add dry elements mixture to the wet elements mixture and stir
    until just combined.
5. Ladle batter into the oil-greased pan and smooth the top.
6. Bake for 45-50 minutes until a tooth-stick comes out clean.
7. Cool for 10 minutes in their pan.

**Prep Time:
15 mins**

**Cook Time:
50 mins**

**Serving
10 slices**

Fluffy Flatbread

Nutrition

Calories: 160 | Protein: 3g | Carbohydrate: 30g | Fat: 4g |
Fiber: 2g

Ingredients

2 cups gluten-free all-purpose flour
1 teaspoon xanthan gum (if not in
flour mix)
1 teaspoon baking powder
½ teaspoon salt
½ cup plain yogurt (dairy or dairy-
free)
¾ cup warm water
1 tablespoon olive oil

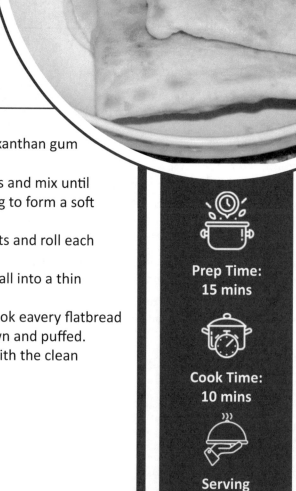

Instructions

1. Take a deep-bottom bowl and toss the flour, xanthan gum
   (if needed), baking powder, and salt.
2. Add yogurt and olive oil to the dry ingredients and mix until
   crumbly. Slowly add warm water while stirring to form a soft
   dough.
3. Divide the dough into 6 same weight segments and roll each
   portion into a ball.
4. On a flour-dusted smooth surface, roll each ball into a thin
   flatbread.
5. Put the nonstick skillet over medium heat. Cook eavery flatbread
   for 2-3 minutes on one side until golden brown and puffed.
6. Transfer the flatbreads to a plate and cover with the clean
   kitchen towel to keep them soft.
7. Serve warm with dips or use as a wrap.

Prep Time:
15 mins

Cook Time:
10 mins

Serving
6 flatbreads

Garlic and Herb Naan

Nutrition

Calories: 180 | Protein: 3g | Carbohydrate: 32g | Fat: 6g |
Fiber: 2g

Ingredients

2 cups gluten-free all-purpose flour
1 teaspoon xanthan gum (if not in
flour mix)
1 teaspoon active dry yeast
½ cup warm water
2 tablespoons olive oil
¼ cup plain yogurt (dairy or dairy-
free)
1 teaspoon salt
1 tablespoon minced garlic
1 tablespoon fresh parsley,
chopped

Instructions

1. Take a small shallow bowl and mix the warm water and
    yeast. Let sit for 5-10 minutes until frothy.
2. Take a deep-bottom bowl and combine flour, xanthan gum (if
    needed), and salt. Toss in the olive oil, yogurt, and yeast mixture
    to form a soft dough.
3. Knead the dough properly for 2-3 minutes, then cover and leave
    for 1 hour.
4. Divide the dough into 6 segments and roll each segments into a
    ball. On a flour-dusted smooth surface, roll each ball into a thin
    circle.
5. Put the nonstick skillet over medium heat. Cook each naan for
    2-3 minutes on one side until golden and puffed.
6. Brush the naan with two tbsp oil and sprinkle with garlic and
    parsley before serving.
7. Serve warm with curry or other dishes.

**Prep Time:
15 mins**

**Cook Time:
10 mins**

**Serving
6 naan**

Buttery Dinner Rolls

Nutrition

Calories: 150 | Protein: 3g | Carbohydrate: 26g | Fat: 4g |
Fiber: 2g

Ingredients

2 ½ cups gluten-free all-purpose
flour
1 teaspoon xanthan gum
1 packet (2 ¼ teaspoons) active dry
yeast
1 ¼ cups warm milk (or dairy-free
alternative)
2 tablespoons honey
1 teaspoon salt
3 tablespoons melted butter (or
coconut oil)
1 large egg

Instructions

1. Take a small shallow bowl and mix the warm milk, honey,
   and yeast. Let it sit for 5-10 minutes until frothy.
2. Take a deep-bottom bowl and combine the flour, xanthan gum (if
   needed), and salt.
3. Add yeast mixture, melted butter, and egg to the dry elements
   and mix until a dough forms.
4. Knead the dough for a few minutes, cover, and put it rise for 1
   hour until doubled in size.
5. Preheat oven to 375°F (190°C). Divide the dough evenly into 12
   portions and roll each into a ball. Place them on a greased baking
   sheet.
6. Bake for 18-20 minutes until golden brown.
7. Brush the rolls with melted butter and serve warm.

**Prep Time:
15 mins**

**Cook Time:
20 mins**

**Serving
12 rolls**

Cinnamon Swirl Breakfast Bread

Nutrition

Calories: 180 | Protein: 4g | Carbohydrate: 30g | Fat: 4g | Fiber: 2g

Ingredients

3 cups gluten-free all-purpose flour
1 teaspoon xanthan gum (if not in flour mix)
1 packet (2 ¼ teaspoons) active dry yeast
1 ¼ cups warm milk (or dairy-free alternative)
¼ cup honey
2 tablespoons butter (or coconut oil)
1 large egg
½ cup coconut sugar
1 tablespoon ground cinnamon

Instructions

1. Take a small shallow bowl and mix the warm milk, honey, and yeast. Let sit for 5-10 minutes until frothy.
2. Take a deep-bottom bowl and combine the flour, xanthan gum (if needed), and salt. Toss in the yeast mixture, melted butter, and egg to form a dough.
3. Knead the dough for a few minutes, cover, and let it rise for 1 hour until doubled in size.
4. Preheat oven to 350°F (175°C). Roll out the dough into a rectangle.
5. Mix the coconut sugar and cinnamon, then sprinkle over the dough. Roll it up tightly and place in a greased loaf pan.
6. Bake for 30-35 minutes until top turns golden and baked thoroughly.
7. Cool the bread for 10 minutes before transferring to the wire rack.

**Prep Time:
20 mins**

**Cook Time:
35 mins**

**Serving
12 slices**

Pies and Tarts

Deep-Dish Apple Pie

Nutrition

Calories: 340 | Protein: 3g | Carbohydrate: 50g | Fat: 16g |
Fiber: 4g

Ingredients

2 ½ cups gluten-free all-purpose
flour
1 teaspoon xanthan gum (if not in
flour mix)
1 cup cold butter (or dairy-free
alternative), cubed
¼ cup ice water
6 large apples (Granny Smith or
Honeycrisp), peeled and sliced
¾ cup coconut sugar
1 teaspoon ground cinnamon
¼ teaspoon ground nutmeg
1 tablespoon lemon juice
1 tablespoon cornstarch

Instructions

1. Grab the deep-bottom bowl and combine gluten-free flour
   and xanthan gum (if needed). Toss in cold butter pieces until the
   mixture resembles coarse crumbs.
2. Gradually add ice water, 1 tbsp at a time, until dough forms.
   Divide in half, shape into disks, wrap in plastic wrap, and
   refrigerate for 30 minutes.
3. Preheat oven to 375°F (190°C). Roll out one dough disk and line
   a deep-dish pie pan.
4. Take a deep-bottom bowl and mix sliced apples, coconut sugar,
   cinnamon, nutmeg, lemon juice, and cornstarch.
5. Ladle apple filling into the prepared crust. Roll out the 2nd
   dough disk and cover the pie, crimping the edges.
6. Make slits in the crust top surface and bake for 50-60 minutes
   until golden brown.
7. Cool the pie for one hour before slicing.

Prep Time:
30 mins

Cook Time:
60 mins

Serving
8 slices

Classic Pumpkin Pie

Nutrition

Calories: 250 | Protein: 4g | Carbohydrate: 36g | Fat: 11g | Fiber: 3g

Ingredients

1 ½ cups gluten-free all-purpose flour
1 teaspoon xanthan gum (if not in flour mix)
½ cup cold butter (or coconut oil), cubed
2 tablespoons ice water
2 cups pumpkin puree
¾ cup coconut sugar
1 teaspoon ground cinnamon
½ teaspoon ground ginger
¼ teaspoon ground nutmeg
¼ teaspoon ground cloves
2 large eggs
1 cup coconut milk (or dairy milk)

Instructions

1. Preheat oven to 350°F (175°C). Grab the deep-bottom bowl and combine flour and xanthan gum (if needed). Cut in butter until crumbly. Add ice water and form into a dough.
2. Roll out the dough and fit it into a 9-inch pie pan. Trim the edges and set aside.
3. Take a deep-bottom bowl and mix pumpkin puree, coconut sugar, cinnamon, ginger, nutmeg, and cloves. Beat in eggs and coconut milk until smooth.
4. Ladle the pumpkin filling into the prepared crust.
5. Bake for 50 minutes or until the filling is set. Leave it aside to cool before serving.
6. Optional: Put whipped cream or coconut cream on top before serving.

Prep Time: 15 mins

Cook Time: 50 mins

Serving 8 slices

Lemon Meringue Tart

Nutrition

Calories: 220 | Protein: 4g | Carbohydrate: 35g | Fat: 8g |
Fiber: 1g

Ingredients

For the crust:
1 ½ cups gluten-free all-purpose flour
1 teaspoon xanthan gum (if not in flour mix)
½ cup cold butter (or dairy-free alternative)
2 tablespoons ice water
For the filling:
1 cup fresh lemon juice
1 tablespoon lemon zest
¾ cup coconut sugar
4 large egg yolks
¼ cup cornstarch
1 ½ cups water
For the meringue:
4 large egg whites
½ teaspoon cream of tartar
½ cup coconut sugar

Instructions

1. Preheat oven to 350°F (175°C). Combine flour and xanthan gum (if needed) for the crust. Cut in cold butter and add ice water to form a dough.
2. Roll out the dough and fit into a 9-inch tart pan. Bake the crust for 10 minutes and leave aside to cool.
3. For the filling, whisk lemon juice, lemon zest, coconut sugar, cornstarch, and water in a saucepan over medium heat until thickened. Remove from heat and toss in egg yolks.
4. Ladle filling into the prepared crust and set aside.
5. To make the meringue, beat egg whites and cream of tartar until soft peaks form. Gradually add sugar and toss until stiff peaks form.
6. Spread meringue over the lemon filling and bake for 12-15 minutes.
7. Let the tart cool before serving.

Prep Time:
25 mins

Cook Time:
35 mins

Serving
8 slices

Blueberry Crumble Pie

Nutrition

Calories: 280 | Protein: 3g | Carbohydrate: 45g | Fat: 11g |
Fiber: 4g

Ingredients

For the crust:
1 ½ cups gluten-free all-purpose flour
1 teaspoon xanthan gum (if not in flour mix)
½ cup cold butter (or coconut oil)
2 tablespoons ice water

For the filling:
4 cups fresh or frozen blueberries
½ cup coconut sugar
1 tablespoon cornstarch
1 tablespoon lemon juice

For the crumble topping:
½ cup gluten-free oats
¼ cup gluten-free flour
¼ cup coconut sugar
¼ cup cold butter (or coconut oil)

Instructions

1. Preheat oven to 375°F (190°C). For the crust, mix the flour and xanthan gum (if needed). Cut in cold butter and add ice water to form a dough.
2. Roll out the dough and fit it into a 9-inch pie pan. Set aside.
3. Take a deep-bottom bowl and mix blueberries, coconut sugar, cornstarch, and lemon juice. Pour the filling into the prepared crust.
4. For the crumble topping, mix oats, flour, and coconut sugar. Cut in cold butter until crumbly. Sprinkle the topping over the blueberry filling.
5. Bake the pie for 40-45 minutes.
6. Cool the pie for one hour, then serve.

**Prep Time:
20mins**

**Cook Time:
45 mins**

**Serving
8 slices**

Southern Peach Pie

Nutrition

Calories: 300 | Protein: 4g | Carbohydrate: 48g | Fat: 11g | Fiber: 3g

Ingredients

For the crust:
2 cups gluten-free all-purpose flour
1 teaspoon xanthan gum (if not in flour mix)
¾ cup cold butter (or coconut oil)
3 tablespoons ice water

For the filling:
5 large peaches, peeled and sliced
¾ cup coconut sugar
1 tablespoon lemon juice
1 teaspoon ground cinnamon
1 tablespoon cornstarch

Instructions

1. Preheat oven to 375°F (190°C). For the crust, mix flour and xanthan gum (if needed). Cut in cold butter and add ice water to form a dough.
2. Roll out half of the dough and line a 9-inch pie pan. Set aside.
3. Take a deep-bottom bowl and mix peaches, coconut sugar, lemon juice, cinnamon, and cornstarch. Pour the filling into the pie crust.
4. Roll out the leftover dough and cover the pie. Crimp the edges and make some slits in the top.
5. Bake for 47-50 minutes until the crust turns golden and the filling begans bubbly.
6. Cool the pie for one hour, then serving.

Prep Time:
20 mins

Cook Time:
50 mins

Serving
8 slices

Key Lime Tart

Nutrition

Calories: 260 | Protein: 5g | Carbohydrate: 34g | Fat: 12g |
Fiber: 1g

Ingredients

For the crust:
1 ½ cups gluten-free graham cracker crumbs
¼ cup melted butter (or coconut oil)
2 tablespoons coconut sugar
For the filling:
½ cup fresh key lime juice
1 tablespoon lime zest
1 can (14 oz) sweetened condensed milk (dairy or dairy-free)
4 large egg yolks

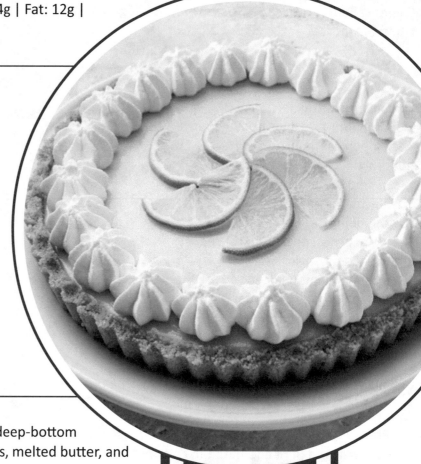

Instructions

1. Preheat oven to 350°F (175°C). Grab the deep-bottom bowl and combine graham cracker crumbs, melted butter, and coconut sugar. Press the mixture softly toward the bottom of a 9-inch tart pan.
2. Bake the crust for 10 minutes.
3. Grab the medium shallow bowl and toss the lime juice, lime zest, condensed milk, and egg yolks until smooth.
4. Pour the filling into the cooled crust.
5. Bake for 15 minutes, then let the tart cool to room temperature.
6. Chill for two hours before serving. Spread whipped cream with lime zest, if desired.

**Prep Time:
20 mins**

**Cook Time:
15 mins**

**Serving
8 slices**

Coconut Cream Pie with Almond Crust

Nutrition

Calories: 310 | Protein: 4g | Carbohydrate: 30g | Fat: 22g |
Fiber: 5g

Ingredients

For the crust:
1 ½ cups almond flour
¼ cup coconut sugar
¼ cup melted coconut oil
For the filling:
1 can (13.5 oz) full-fat coconut milk
¾ cup coconut sugar
¼ cup cornstarch
½ teaspoon vanilla extract
1 cup shredded unsweetened coconut
For the topping:
1 cup coconut whipped cream (or
regular whipped cream)
¼ cup toasted coconut flakes

Instructions

1. Preheat oven to 350°F (175°C). Grab the deep-bottom bowl and combine almond flour, coconut sugar, and melted coconut oil. Press into a 9-inch pie pan.
2. Bake the crust for 10-12 minutes until golden. Let it cool.
3. In a saucepan, toss the coconut milk, coconut sugar, and cornstarch. Cook over moderate flame, stirring constantly, until thickened (about 10 minutes).
4. Remove from heat and toss in vanilla extract and shredded coconut. Pour the filling into the cooled crust.
5. Refrigerate for at least 2 hours until set.
6. Spread whipped cream and toasted coconut flakes on top before serving.

**Prep Time:
20 mins**

**Cook Time:
20 mins**

**Serving
8 slices**

Zesty Lemon Curd Tart

Nutrition

Calories: 280 | Protein: 4g | Carbohydrate: 30g | Fat: 18g | Fiber: 1g

Ingredients

For the crust:
1 ½ cups gluten-free all-purpose flour
1 teaspoon xanthan gum (if not in flour mix)
½ cup cold butter (or coconut oil), cubed
2 tablespoons ice water

For the filling:
½ cup fresh lemon juice
1 tablespoon lemon zest
½ cup coconut sugar
4 large egg yolks
¼ cup butter (or coconut oil), melted

Instructions

1. Preheat oven to 350°F (175°C). Grab the deep-bottom bowl and mix the flour and xanthan gum (if needed). Add cold butter pieces until the mixture resembles coarse crumbs. Add ice water to form a dough.
2. Roll out the dough and fit into a 9-inch tart pan. Bake the crust for 8-10 minutes. Leave it aside to cool.
3. In a medium saucepan, toss the lemon juice, lemon zest, coconut sugar, and egg yolks. Cook over low flame, stirring, until the mixture thickens (about 10 minutes).
4. Remove and toss in melted butter until smooth.
5. Spread the lemon curd over cooled crust and refrigerate for at least 2 hours.
6. Garnish with extra lemon zest before serving.

**Prep Time:
20 mins**

**Cook Time:
15 mins**

**Serving
8 slices**

Dark Chocolate Ganache Tart

Nutrition

Calories: 290 | Protein: 3g | Carbohydrate: 24g | Fat: 21g | Fiber: 3g

Ingredients

For the crust:
1 ½ cups gluten-free chocolate cookie crumbs
¼ cup melted butter (or coconut oil)

For the filling:
1 cup dark chocolate chips
½ cup full-fat coconut milk
1 teaspoon vanilla extract

Instructions

1. Preheat oven to 350°F (175°C). Toss the chocolate cookie crumbs with melted butter and press toward the bottom of a 9-inch tart pan. Bake for 10 minutes and leave aside to cool.
2. In a small shallow pan, heat the coconut milk until it begins to simmer.
3. Pour the hot coconut milk over the dark chocolate chips and put it aside for 2 minutes. Stir until smooth and fully melted. Add vanilla extract and stir to combine.
4. Pour the ganache filling into the cooled crust.
5. Refrigerate the tart for at least 4 hours or until the ganache is set.
6. Garnish with shaved chocolate or berries before serving.

Prep Time:
15 mins

Cook Time:
10 mins

Serving
8 slices

Almond and Apricot Tart

Nutrition

Calories: 290 | Protein: 6g | Carbohydrate: 24g | Fat: 20g |
Fiber: 4g

Ingredients

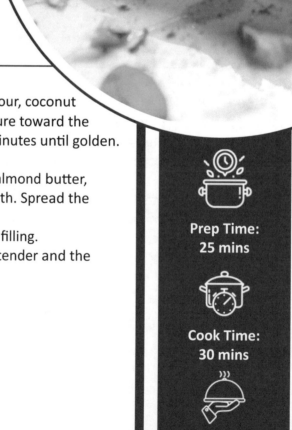

For the crust:
1 ½ cups almond flour
¼ cup coconut sugar
¼ cup melted coconut oil
For the filling:
½ cup almond butter
¼ cup coconut sugar
1 tablespoon almond extract
12 fresh apricots, halved and pitted

Instructions

1. Preheat oven to 350°F (175°C). Mix almond flour, coconut
   sugar, and melted coconut oil. Press the mixture toward the
   bottom of a 9-inch tart pan. Bake for 10-12 minutes until golden.
   Leave it aside to cool.
2. Grab the medium shallow bowl and toss the almond butter,
   coconut sugar, and almond extract until smooth. Spread the
   almond mixture evenly over the cooled crust.
3. Arrange apricots halves on top of the almond filling.
4. Bake for 25-30 minutes until the apricots are tender and the
   filling is set.
5. Let the tart cool before serving.

Prep Time:
25 mins

Cook Time:
30 mins

Serving
8 slices

Cakes, Cupcakes, and Muffins

Decadent Chocolate Layer Cake

Nutrition

Calories: 320 | Protein: 5g | Carbohydrate: 40g | Fat: 18g | Fiber: 4g

Ingredients

For the cake:
2 cups gluten-free all-purpose flour
1 teaspoon xanthan gum
¾ cup cocoa powder
1 ½ teaspoons baking soda
1 teaspoon baking powder
½ teaspoon salt
1 ½ cups coconut sugar
1 cup milk (or dairy-free alternative)
½ cup melted coconut oil
2 large eggs
1 teaspoon vanilla extract
1 cup hot water

For the frosting:
1 cup dairy-free chocolate chips
½ cup full-fat coconut milk
1 teaspoon vanilla extract

Instructions

1. Preheat oven to 350°F (175°C). Grease and arrange two 9-inch round cake pans.
2. Take a deep-bottom bowl and toss the flour, xanthan gum, cocoa powder, baking soda, baking powder, salt, and coconut sugar.
3. Take the other shallow bowl and toss the milk, melted coconut oil with eggs, and vanilla extract.
4. Gradually add the wet elements mixture to the dry elements mixture, mixing until smooth. Toss in the hot water.
5. Divide the batter between the two greased and arranged pans and bake for 25-30 minutes until a tooth-stick is inserted and comes out clean. Let the cakes cool completely.
6. For the frosting, heat the coconut milk and pour it over the chocolate chips. Put it aside for 2 minutes, then stir until smooth. Toss in vanilla extract.
7. Once the cakes have cooled, frost between the layers and over the top and sides of the cake.

**Prep Time:
15 mins**

**Cook Time:
30 mins**

**Serving
12 slices**

Vanilla Sponge Cake with Fresh Berries

Nutrition

Calories: 220 | Protein: 4g | Carbohydrate: 30g | Fat: 10g |
Fiber: 2g

Ingredients

1 ½ cups gluten-free all-purpose
flour
1 teaspoon xanthan gum
1 teaspoon baking powder
½ teaspoon baking soda
½ teaspoon salt
¾ cup coconut sugar
½ cup melted butter (or coconut
oil)
3 large eggs
1 teaspoon vanilla extract
½ cup milk (or dairy-free
alternative)
1 cup fresh mixed berries
(blueberries, raspberries, etc.)

Instructions

1. Preheat oven to 350°F (175°C). Grease and arrange an
   8-inch round cake pan.
2. Grab the medium shallow bowl and toss the flour with xanthan
   gum, baking powder, baking soda, and salt.
3. Take the other shallow bowl and toss the coconut sugar, melted
   butter, eggs, vanilla extract, and milk until smooth.
4. Add dry ingredients in small portions to the wet mixture and stir
   until combined.
5. Ladle batter into the greased and arranged cake pan and bake
   for 20-25 minutes until a tooth-stick is inserted and comes out
   clean. Let the cake cool.
6. Top the cooled cake with fresh mixed berries before serving.

**Prep Time:
5 mins**

**Cook Time:
25 mins**

**Serving
12 slices**

Zesty Lemon Drizzle Cake

Nutrition

Calories: 200 | Protein: 3g | Carbohydrate: 30g | Fat: 9g | Fiber: 2g

Ingredients

For the cake:
1 ½ cups gluten-free all-purpose flour
1 teaspoon xanthan gum
1 teaspoon baking powder
½ teaspoon baking soda
½ teaspoon salt
¾ cup coconut sugar
½ cup melted coconut oil
2 large eggs
1 teaspoon vanilla extract
1 tablespoon lemon zest
¼ cup fresh lemon juice
½ cup milk (or dairy-free alternative)
For the drizzle:
¼ cup fresh lemon juice
¼ cup coconut sugar

Instructions

1. Preheat oven to 350°F (175°C). Grease a loaf pan.
2. Grab the deep-bottom bowl and toss the flour with xanthan gum, baking powder, coconut sugar, baking soda, and salt.
3. In another deep-bottom bowl, toss the melted coconut oil with eggs, vanilla, lemon zest, lemon juice, and milk.
4. Gradually combine the wet elements mixture with the dry elements mixture and stir until smooth.
5. Ladle batter into the oil greased pan and bake for 35-40 minutes until a tooth-stick is inserted and comes out clean.
6. For the drizzle, toss the lemon juice with coconut sugar until dissolved. Drizzle over the warm cake, then put aside to cool completely before slicing.

Prep Time:
15 mins

Cook Time:
40 mins

Serving
10 slices

Red Velvet Cake with Cream Frosting

Nutrition

Calories: 280 | Protein: 5g | Carbohydrate: 34g | Fat: 14g | Fiber: 2g

Ingredients

For the cake:
2 cups gluten-free all-purpose flour
1 teaspoon xanthan gum
1 teaspoon baking soda
1 tablespoon cocoa powder
½ teaspoon salt
1 cup coconut sugar
1 cup buttermilk (or dairy-free milk with 1 tablespoon vinegar)
½ cup melted coconut oil
2 large eggs
1 teaspoon vanilla extract
1 tablespoon red food coloring
For the frosting:
1 ½ cups dairy-free cream cheese
½ cup coconut sugar
1 teaspoon vanilla extract

Instructions

1. Preheat oven to 350°F (175°C). Grease two 9-inch round cake pans.
2. Take a deep-bottom bowl and mix the flour, xanthan gum, baking soda, cocoa powder, salt, and coconut sugar.
3. In another deep-bottom bowl, toss the buttermilk, melted coconut oil with eggs, vanilla extract, and red food coloring.
4. Slowly add the wet elements mixture to the dry elements mixture, stirring until smooth.
5. Ladle batter between the two cake pans and bake for 25-30 minutes. Let the cakes cool completely.
6. For the frosting, mix the dairy-free cream cheese, coconut sugar, and vanilla extract until smooth. Frost between the cake layers and over the top and sides.

Prep Time:
20 mins

Cook Time:
30 mins

Serving
12 slices

Cinnamon Coffee Cake

Nutrition

Calories: 240 | Protein: 4g | Carbohydrate: 34g | Fat: 10g | Fiber: 2g

Ingredients

For the cake:
1 ½ cups gluten-free all-purpose flour
1 teaspoon xanthan gum
1 teaspoon baking powder
½ teaspoon baking soda
½ teaspoon salt
½ cup coconut sugar
½ cup melted butter (or coconut oil)
2 large eggs
1 teaspoon vanilla extract
½ cup milk (or dairy-free alternative)

For the cinnamon swirl:
½ cup coconut sugar
1 tablespoon ground cinnamon
2 tablespoons melted butter

Instructions

1. Preheat oven to 350°F (175°C). Grease a 9-inch cake pan.
2. Grab the deep-bottom bowl and toss the flour with xanthan gum, baking powder, coconut sugar, baking soda and salt.
3. In another deep-bottom bowl, toss the melted butter, eggs, vanilla extract, and milk. Gradually add wet ingredients to the dry and mix until smooth.
4. Take a small shallow bowl and combine the coconut sugar, cinnamon, and melted butter for the swirl.
5. Ladle cake batter (add half) into the prepared pan, sprinkle the cinnamon mixture over it, then pour the remaining batter on top.
6. Bake for 30-35 minutes until a tooth-stick is inserted and comes out clean. Leave it aside to cool before serving.

**Prep Time:
20 mins**

**Cook Time:
35 mins**

**Serving
10 slices**

Marbled Chocolate and Vanilla Cake

Nutrition

Calories: 230 | Protein: 4g | Carbohydrate: 30g | Fat: 10g | Fiber: 2g

Ingredients

1 ½ cups gluten-free all-purpose flour
1 teaspoon xanthan gum
1 teaspoon baking powder
½ teaspoon baking soda
½ teaspoon salt
1 cup coconut sugar
½ cup melted butter (or coconut oil)
2 large eggs
1 teaspoon vanilla extract
½ cup milk (or dairy-free alternative)
¼ cup cocoa powder
¼ cup hot water

Instructions

1. Preheat oven to 350°F (175°C). Grease a 9-inch loaf pan.
2. Grab the deep-bottom bowl and mix flour, xanthan gum, baking powder, baking soda, salt, and coconut sugar.
3. In another deep-bottom bowl, toss the melted butter, eggs, vanilla, and milk. Gradually add wet elements mixture to the dry elements mixture and stir until smooth.
4. Divide the batter in half. In one half, mix the cocoa powder and hot water until smooth.
5. Pour alternating spoonfuls of the vanilla and chocolate batters into the prepared pan to create a marbled effect. Swirl lightly with a knife for a more defined marble look.
6. Bake for 30-35 minutes or until a tooth-stick is inserted and comes out clean. Leave it aside to cool before slicing.

**Prep Time:
20 mins**

**Cook Time:
35 mins**

**Serving
12 slices**

Almond Flour Orange Cake

Nutrition

Calories: 250 | Protein: 6g | Carbohydrate: 16g | Fat: 18g |
Fiber: 4g

Ingredients

2 cups almond flour
½ cup coconut sugar
1 teaspoon baking powder
½ teaspoon baking soda
¼ teaspoon salt
3 large eggs
½ cup melted coconut oil
2 tablespoons orange zest
¼ cup fresh orange juice
1 teaspoon vanilla extract

Instructions

1. Preheat oven to 350°F (175°C). Grease a 9-inch round cake pan.
2. Grab the medium shallow bowl and mix almond flour with coconut sugar, baking powder, baking soda, and salt.
3. Take the other shallow bowl and toss the eggs, melted coconut oil, orange zest, orange juice, and vanilla extract.
4. Add the wet elements mixture to the dry elements mixture and stir until combined.
5. Ladle batter into the greased cake pan and bake for 35-40 minutes until a tooth-stick is inserted and comes out clean.
6. Let the cake cool before shifting to a wire rack to cool completely.

**Prep Time:
15 mins**

**Cook Time:
40 mins**

**Serving
10 slices**

Molten Chocolate Lava Cake

Nutrition

Calories: 300 | Protein: 4g | Carbohydrate: 32g | Fat: 18g | Fiber: 3g

Ingredients

½ cup dairy-free chocolate chips
¼ cup melted coconut oil
2 large eggs
½ cup coconut sugar
¼ cup gluten-free all-purpose flour
1 teaspoon vanilla extract
Pinch of salt

Instructions

1. Preheat oven to 425°F (220°C). Grease six ramekins.
2. Melt the chocolate chips with coconut oil (you can use microwave or double boiler until smooth).
3. Take the other shallow bowl and toss the eggs with coconut sugar until light and fluffy.
4. Beat the melted chocolate mixture with egg mixture. Add flour, vanilla extract, and salt, stirring until combined.
5. Ladle batter evenly among the greased ramekins.
6. Bake for 10-12 minutes until the edges are set but the centers are still soft.
7. Put the cakes aside to cool for 1 minute before gently turning them out onto plates. Serve warmly.

Prep Time:
10 mins

Cook Time:
12 mins

Serving
6 mini cakes

Chocolate Fudge Cupcakes

Nutrition

Calories: 280 | Protein: 4g | Carbohydrate: 30g | Fat: 16g | Fiber: 3g

Ingredients

For the cupcakes:
1 ½ cups gluten-free all-purpose flour
1 teaspoon xanthan gum
½ cup cocoa powder
1 teaspoon baking powder
½ teaspoon baking soda
½ teaspoon salt
1 cup coconut sugar
½ cup melted coconut oil
2 large eggs
1 teaspoon vanilla extract
½ cup milk (or dairy-free alternative)
For the frosting:
1 cup dairy-free chocolate chips
½ cup full-fat coconut milk

Instructions

1. Preheat oven to 350°F (175°C). Arrange the 12-cup muffin tin with paper liners.
2. Take a deep-bottom bowl and toss the flour with xanthan gum, cocoa powder, baking powder, baking soda, salt, and coconut sugar.
3. In another deep-bottom bowl, toss the melted coconut oil with eggs, vanilla extract, and milk. Add wet ingredients to the dryer and mix until smooth.
4. Ladle batter evenly among the cupcake liners. Bake for 18-20 minutes until a tooth-stick is inserted and comes out clean. Leave it aside to cool completely.
5. For the frosting, heat the coconut milk, then drizzle it over the chocolate chips. Stir until smooth and refrigerate for 1 hour to thicken. Spread the frosting over the cooled cupcakes.

**Prep Time:
15 mins**

**Cook Time:
20 mins**

**Serving
12 cupcakes**

Vanilla Almond Cupcakes

Nutrition

Calories: 250 | Protein: 5g | Carbohydrate: 20g | Fat: 18g |
Fiber: 3g

Ingredients

For the cupcakes:
1 ½ cups almond flour
½ cup coconut sugar
1 teaspoon baking powder
½ teaspoon baking soda
¼ teaspoon salt
3 large eggs
½ cup melted coconut oil
1 teaspoon vanilla extract
½ cup milk (or dairy-free
alternative)
For the frosting:
1 cup dairy-free cream cheese
½ cup coconut sugar
1 teaspoon almond extract

Instructions

1. Preheat oven to 350°F (175°C). Arrange the 12-cup muffin
   tin with paper liners.
2. Grab the medium shallow bowl and mix almond flour with
   coconut sugar, baking powder, baking soda, and salt.
3. Take the other shallow bowl and toss the eggs, melted coconut
   oil, vanilla extract, and milk. Add wet elements mixture to the
   dry elements mixture and stir until smooth.
4. Ladle batter evenly among the cupcake liners. Bake for 18-20
   minutes until a tooth-stick is inserted and comes out clean.
   Leave it aside to cool completely.
5. For the frosting, mix cream cheese, coconut sugar, and almond
   extract until smooth. Frost the cooled cupcakes before serving.

Prep Time:
15 mins

Cook Time:
20 mins

Serving
12 cupcakes

Lemon Poppy Seed Muffins

Nutrition

Calories: 180 | Protein: 3g | Carbohydrate: 23g | Fat: 9g |
Fiber: 2g

Ingredients

1 ½ cups gluten-free all-purpose
flour
1 teaspoon xanthan gum
1 teaspoon baking powder
½ teaspoon baking soda
¼ teaspoon salt
½ cup coconut sugar
½ cup melted coconut oil
2 large eggs
2 tablespoons lemon zest
¼ cup fresh lemon juice
1 teaspoon vanilla extract
2 tablespoons poppy seeds
½ cup milk (or dairy-free
alternative)

Instructions

1. Preheat oven to 350°F (175°C). Arrange the muffin tin with paper liners.
2. Grab the medium shallow bowl and toss the flour with xanthan gum, baking powder, coconut sugar, baking soda and salt.
3. Take the other shallow bowl and mix melted coconut oil with eggs, lemon zest, lemon juice, vanilla, and milk.
4. Gradually add the wet elements mixture to the dry elements mixture, stirring until just combined. Fold in the poppy seeds.
5. Ladle batter evenly among the muffin cups.
6. Bake for 18-20 minutes or until a tooth-stick is inserted and comes out clean. Leave it aside to cool before serving.

**Prep Time:
15 mins**

**Cook Time:
20 mins**

**Serving
12 muffins**

Blueberry Oat Muffins

Nutrition

Calories: 210 | Protein: 4g | Carbohydrate: 30g | Fat: 9g | Fiber: 3g

Ingredients

1 ½ cups gluten-free oats
1 cup gluten-free all-purpose flour
1 teaspoon xanthan gum
1 teaspoon baking powder
½ teaspoon baking soda
½ teaspoon cinnamon
¼ teaspoon salt
½ cup coconut sugar
½ cup melted coconut oil
2 large eggs
1 teaspoon vanilla extract
½ cup milk (or dairy-free alternative)
1 cup fresh or frozen blueberries

Instructions

1. Preheat oven to 350°F (175°C). Arrange the muffin tin with paper liners.
2. Grab the medium shallow bowl and mix oats, flour with xanthan gum, baking powder, baking soda, cinnamon powder, salt, and coconut sugar.
3. Take the other shallow bowl and toss the melted coconut oil with eggs, vanilla extract, and milk.
4. Add the wet elements mixture to the dry elements mixture and stir until it is combined. Gently fold in the blueberries.
5. Ladle batter evenly among the muffin cups.
6. Bake for 22-25 minutes or until a tooth-stick is inserted and comes out clean. Leave it aside to cool before serving.

**Prep Time:
15 mins**

**Cook Time:
25 mins**

**Serving
12 muffins**

Double Chocolate Chip Muffins

Nutrition

Calories: 220 | Protein: 4g | Carbohydrate: 30g | Fat: 11g |
Fiber: 3g

Ingredients

1 ½ cups gluten-free all-purpose
flour
1 teaspoon xanthan gum
½ cup cocoa powder
1 teaspoon baking powder
½ teaspoon baking soda
¼ teaspoon salt
½ cup coconut sugar
½ cup melted coconut oil
2 large eggs
1 teaspoon vanilla extract
½ cup milk (or dairy-free
alternative)
½ cup dairy-free chocolate chips

Instructions

1. Preheat oven to 350°F (175°C). Arrange the muffin tin with
   paper liners.
2. Grab the medium shallow bowl and mix flour with xanthan gum,
   cocoa powder, baking powder, baking soda, salt, and coconut
   sugar.
3. Take the other shallow bowl and toss the melted coconut oil
   with eggs, vanilla extract, and milk.
4. Add the wet elements mixture to the dry elements mixture and
   stir until combined. Fold in the chocolate chips.
5. Ladle batter evenly among the muffin cups.
6. Bake for 18-20 minutes until a tooth-stick is inserted and comes
   out clean. Leave it aside to cool before serving.

Prep Time:
15 mins

Cook Time:
20 mins

**Serving
12 muffins**

Banana Walnut Muffins

Nutrition

Calories: 210 | Protein: 4g | Carbohydrate: 28g | Fat: 10g | Fiber: 3g

Ingredients

1 ½ cups gluten-free all-purpose flour
1 teaspoon xanthan gum
1 teaspoon baking powder
½ teaspoon baking soda
¼ teaspoon salt
½ cup coconut sugar
½ cup melted coconut oil
2 large eggs
2 ripe bananas, mashed
1 teaspoon vanilla extract
½ cup chopped walnuts

Instructions

1. Preheat oven to 350°F (175°C). Arrange the muffin tin with paper liners.
2. Grab the medium shallow bowl and toss the flour with xanthan gum, baking powder, baking soda, salt, and coconut sugar.
3. Take the other shallow bowl and toss the melted coconut oil with eggs, mashed bananas, and vanilla extract.
4. Add the wet elements mixture to the dry elements mixture and stir until it is combined. Fold in the chopped walnuts.
5. Ladle batter evenly among the muffin cups.
6. Bake for 18-20 minutes or until a tooth-stick is inserted and comes out clean. Leave it aside to cool before serving.

Prep Time:
15 mins

Cook Time:
20 mins

Serving
12 muffins

Cornmeal Muffins with Honey Butter

Nutrition

Calories: 230 | Protein: 4g | Carbohydrate: 28g | Fat: 11g |
Fiber: 2g

Ingredients

For the muffins:
1 cup gluten-free cornmeal
1 cup gluten-free all-purpose flour
1 teaspoon xanthan gum
1 tablespoon baking powder
½ teaspoon salt
½ cup coconut sugar
½ cup melted butter (or coconut oil)
2 large eggs
1 cup milk (or dairy-free alternative)
For the honey butter:
½ cup softened butter (or dairy-free alternative)
2 tablespoons honey

Instructions

1. Preheat oven to 350°F (175°C). Arrange the muffin tin with paper liners.
2. Grab the medium shallow bowl and toss the cornmeal, flour, xanthan gum, baking powder, salt, and coconut sugar.
3. Take the other shallow bowl and toss the melted butter, eggs, and milk.
4. Gradually add the wet elements mixture to the dry elements mixture and stir until it is combined.
5. Ladle batter evenly among the muffin cups.
6. Bake for 18-20 minutes or until a tooth-stick is inserted and comes out clean. Leave it aside to cool before serving.
7. For the honey butter, mix softened butter and honey until smooth. Serve alongside the muffins.

**Prep Time:
15 mins**

**Cook Time:
20 mins**

**Serving
12 muffins**

Cookies and Bars

Chewy Chocolate Chip Cookies

Nutrition

Calories: 150 | Protein: 2g | Carbohydrate: 20g | Fat: 8g | Fiber: 1g

Ingredients

2 cups gluten-free all-purpose flour
1 teaspoon xanthan gum
1 teaspoon baking soda
½ teaspoon salt
1 cup coconut sugar
½ cup melted coconut oil
2 large eggs
1 teaspoon vanilla extract
1 ½ cups dairy-free chocolate chips

Instructions

1. Preheat oven to 350°F (175°C). Arrange the baking sheet with parchment paper.
2. Grab the deep-bottom bowl and toss the flour, xanthan gum, baking soda, and salt.
3. Take the other shallow bowl and mix coconut sugar, melted coconut oil with eggs, and vanilla extract.
4. Gradually add dry elements mixture to the wet elements mixture, mixing until combined. Fold in the chocolate chips.
5. Drop fully loaded tablespoon balls of dough onto the parchment paper-arranged baking sheet, spacing them 2 inches apart.
6. Bake for 10-12 minutes until the around edges turn golden but soft in the center.
7. Leave it aside to cool on the baking sheet for 5 minutes to cool completely.

Prep Time:
15 mins

Cook Time:
12 mins

Serving
24 cookies

Oatmeal Raisin Cookies

Nutrition

Calories: 130 | Protein: 2g | Carbohydrate: 18g | Fat: 6g |
Fiber: 2g

Ingredients

1 ½ cups gluten-free oats
1 cup gluten-free all-purpose flour
1 teaspoon xanthan gum
1 teaspoon baking soda
½ teaspoon cinnamon
½ teaspoon salt
½ cup coconut sugar
½ cup melted coconut oil
2 large eggs
1 teaspoon vanilla extract
¾ cup raisins

Instructions

1. Preheat oven to 350°F (175°C). Arrange the baking sheet with parchment paper.
2. Grab the deep-bottom bowl and mix oats, flour, xanthan gum, baking soda, cinnamon, and salt.
3. Take the other shallow bowl and toss the coconut sugar, melted coconut oil with eggs, and vanilla extract.
4. Gradually add dry elements mixture to the wet elements mixture, stirring until combined. Fold in the raisins.
5. Drop fully loaded tablespoon balls of dough onto the parchment paper-arranged baking sheet, spacing them 2 inches apart.
6. Bake for 10-12 minutes until golden brown.
7. Leave it aside to cool on the baking sheet for 5 minutes to cool completely.

Prep Time:
15 mins

Cook Time:
12 mins

Serving
24 cookies

Peanut Butter and Chocolate Cookies

Nutrition

Calories: 130 | Protein: 4g | Carbohydrate: 10g | Fat: 9g |
Fiber: 2g

Ingredients

1 cup natural peanut butter (unsweetened)
½ cup coconut sugar
1 large egg
1 teaspoon vanilla extract
½ teaspoon baking soda
½ cup dairy-free chocolate chips

Instructions

1. Preheat oven to 350°F (175°C). Arrange the baking sheet
   with parchment paper.
2. Grab the medium shallow bowl and mix the peanut butter,
   coconut sugar, egg, vanilla extract, and baking soda until smooth.
3. Fold in the chocolate chips.
4. Drop fully loaded tablespoon balls of dough onto the parchmnet
   paper-arranged baking sheet, spacing them 2 inches apart.
   Flatten slightly with a fork.
5. Bake for 8-10 minutes.
6. Leave it aside to cool on the baking sheet for 5 minutes to cool
   completely.

Prep Time:
10 mins

Cook Time:
10 mins

Serving
24 cookies

Butter Shortbread Cookies

Nutrition

Calories: 110 | Protein: 1g | Carbohydrate: 12g | Fat: 7g |
Fiber: 1g

Ingredients

2 cups gluten-free all-purpose flour
1 teaspoon xanthan gum
½ cup coconut sugar
1 cup cold butter (or dairy-free
alternative)
1 teaspoon vanilla extract

Instructions

1. Preheat oven to 325°F (165°C). Arrange the baking sheet
   with parchment paper.
2. Grab the deep-bottom bowl and mix the flour, xanthan gum, and
   coconut sugar.
3. Cut the cold butter into the flour mixture until it forms coarse
   crumbs. Add vanilla extract and mix until a dough forms.
4. Roll out the dough on the flour-dusted smooth surface to ¼-inch
   thickness. Cut out cookies with a cookie cutter and place them
   on the parchment paper-arranged baking sheet.
5. Bake for 10-12 minutes. Leave it aside to cool on the baking
   sheet for 5 minutes to cool completely.

Prep Time:
15 mins

Cook Time:
12 mins

Serving
24 cookies

Gingerbread Men Cookies

Nutrition

Calories: 120 | Protein: 2g | Carbohydrate: 20g | Fat: 4g |
Fiber: 1g

Ingredients

2 ½ cups gluten-free all-purpose
flour
1 teaspoon xanthan gum
1 teaspoon baking soda
½ teaspoon salt
2 teaspoons ground ginger
1 teaspoon ground cinnamon
½ teaspoon ground cloves
½ cup coconut sugar
½ cup melted coconut oil
1 large egg
½ cup molasses
1 teaspoon vanilla extract

Instructions

1. Take a deep-bottom bowl and mix flour, xanthan gum, baking soda, salt, ginger, cinnamon, cloves, and coconut sugar.
2. Take the other shallow bowl and toss the melted coconut oil with egg, molasses, and vanilla extract.
3. Gradually add wet elements mixture to the dry elements mixture and mix until a dough forms. Wrap the dough and chill for 1 hour.
4. Preheat oven to 350°F (175°C). Arrange the baking sheet with parchment paper.
5. Roll out the dough on the flour-dusted smooth surface to ¼-inch thickness. Cut out gingerbread men's shapes and place them on the baking sheet.
6. Bake for 8-10 minutes until firm. Leave it aside to cool on the baking sheet for 5 minutes to cool completely.
7. Decorate with icing, if desired.

**Prep Time:
20 mins**

**Cook Time:
10 mins**

**Serving
24 cookies**

Raspberry Thumbprint Cookies

Nutrition

Calories: 100 | Protein: 1g | Carbohydrate: 12g | Fat: 5g |
Fiber: 1g

Ingredients

1 ½ cups gluten-free all-purpose
flour
1 teaspoon xanthan gum
½ teaspoon baking powder
¼ teaspoon salt
½ cup coconut sugar
½ cup melted coconut oil
1 large egg
1 teaspoon vanilla extract
½ cup raspberry jam (sugar-free or
regular)

Instructions

1. Preheat oven to 350°F (175°C). Arrange the baking sheet
   with parchment paper.
2. Grab the medium shallow bowl and toss the flour, xanthan gum,
   baking powder, salt, and coconut sugar.
3. Take the other shallow bowl and mix melted coconut oil with
   egg, and vanilla extract. Gradually add wet elements mixture to
   the dry elements mixture and mix until combined.
4. Roll fully loaded tablespoon of dough and place them on the
   parchment paper-arranged baking sheet. Use your thumb to
   create an indentation in the center of each cookie.
5. Spoon a small amount of raspberry jam into each indentation.
6. Bake for 10-12 minutes until lightly golden. Leave it aside to cool
   on the baking sheet for 5 minutes.

**Prep Time:
10 mins**

**Cook Time:
12 mins**

**Serving
24 cookies**

Almond Flour Biscuit Cookies

Nutrition

Calories: 110 | Protein: 3g | Carbohydrate: 7g | Fat: 8g |
Fiber: 2g

Ingredients

2 cups almond flour
½ cup coconut sugar
1 teaspoon baking powder
¼ teaspoon salt
1 large egg
¼ cup melted coconut oil
1 teaspoon vanilla extract

Instructions

1. Preheat oven to 350°F (175°C). Arrange the baking sheet with parchment paper.
2. Take a deep-bottom bowl and mix almond flour with coconut sugar, baking powder, and salt.
3. Take the other shallow bowl and toss the egg, melted coconut oil, and vanilla extract.
4. Add wet elements mixture to the dry elements mixture and mix until combined.
5. Roll fully loaded tablespoon of dough and place them on the parchment paper-arranged baking sheet. Flatten slightly with your hand.
6. Bake for 10-12 minutes. Cool the cookies for 5 minutes.

**Prep Time:
10 mins**

**Cook Time:
12 mins**

**Serving
24 cookies**

Lemon Zest Bars

Nutrition

Calories: 170 | Protein: 3g | Carbohydrate: 25g | Fat: 7g | Fiber: 1g

Ingredients

For the crust:
1 ½ cups gluten-free all-purpose flour
1 teaspoon xanthan gum
½ cup cold butter (or dairy-free alternative)
¼ cup coconut sugar
For the filling:
3 large eggs
¾ cup coconut sugar
¼ cup gluten-free all-purpose flour
2 tablespoons lemon zest
½ cup fresh lemon juice

Instructions

1. Preheat oven to 350°F (175°C). Grease an 8x8-inch baking pan.
2. For the crust, mix flour, xanthan gum, and coconut sugar. Toss in cold butter pieces until the mixture resembles coarse crumbs.
3. Press the crust mixture toward the bottom of the greased pan. Bake for 15 minutes until lightly golden.
4. For the filling, toss the eggs, coconut sugar, flour, lemon zest, and lemon juice until smooth.
5. Ladle filling over the pre-baked crust and bake for another 20 minutes until set.
6. Cool the bars completely, then make into squares.

Prep Time:
15 mins

Cook Time:
35 mins

Serving
12 bars

Fudgy Brownie Squares

Nutrition

Calories: 190 | Protein: 3g | Carbohydrate: 25g | Fat: 10g |
Fiber: 2g

Ingredients

1 ½ cups gluten-free all-purpose
flour
1 teaspoon xanthan gum
½ cup cocoa powder
1 teaspoon baking powder
½ teaspoon salt
¾ cup coconut sugar
½ cup melted coconut oil
2 large eggs
1 teaspoon vanilla extract
½ cup dairy-free chocolate chips

Instructions

1. Preheat oven to 350°F (175°C). Grease an 8x8-inch baking
   pan.
2. Take a deep-bottom bowl and toss the flour, xanthan gum, cocoa
   powder, baking powder, salt, and coconut sugar.
3. Take the other shallow bowl and mix melted coconut oil with
   eggs and vanilla extract.
4. Gradually add wet elements mixture to the dry elements mixture
   and stir until combined. Fold in the chocolate chips.
5. Ladle batter into the prepared pan. Bake for 22-25 minutes until
   a tooth-stick is inserted comes out with moist crumbs.
6. Cool the brownies before slicing them into squares.

**Prep Time:
10 mins**

**Cook Time:
25 mins**

**Serving
12 squares**

Butterscotch Blondie Bars

Nutrition

Calories: 200 | Protein: 3g | Carbohydrate: 28g | Fat: 9g |
Fiber: 1g

Ingredients

1 ½ cups gluten-free all-purpose
flour
1 teaspoon xanthan gum
½ teaspoon baking powder
¼ teaspoon salt
¾ cup coconut sugar
½ cup melted butter (or coconut
oil)
2 large eggs
1 teaspoon vanilla extract
½ cup butterscotch chips (dairy-
free, if needed)

Instructions

1. Preheat oven to 350°F (175°C). Grease an 8x8-inch baking
   pan.
2. Take a deep-bottom bowl and toss the flour with xanthan gum,
   coconut sugar, baking powder, and salt.
3. Take the other shallow bowl and mix melted butter, eggs, and
   vanilla extract.
4. Gradually add wet elements mixture to the dry elements mixture
   and stir until combined. Fold in the butterscotch chips.
5. Ladle batter into the greased pan and bake for 20-25 minutes
   until golden brown.
6. Cool the blondies before slicing into bars.

**Prep Time:
10 mins**

**Cook Time:
25 mins**

**Serving
12 bars**

Cranberry Almond Biscotti

Nutrition

Calories: 150 | Protein: 4g | Carbohydrate: 18g | Fat: 8g |
Fiber: 2g

Ingredients

1 ½ cups almond flour
½ cup gluten-free all-purpose flour
½ teaspoon xanthan gum (if not in
flour mix)
1 teaspoon baking powder
¼ teaspoon salt
½ cup coconut sugar
2 large eggs
1 teaspoon vanilla extract
½ cup dried cranberries
½ cup sliced almonds

Instructions

1. Preheat oven to 350°F (175°C). Arrange the baking sheet
   with parchment paper.
2. Grab the medium shallow bowl and mix almond flour with all-
   purpose flour, xanthan gum, coconut sugar, baking powder, and
   salt.
3. Take the other shallow bowl and toss the eggs and vanilla
   extract. Gradually add wet elements mixture to the dry elements
   mixture, mixing until a dough forms. Fold in the cranberries and
   almonds.
4. Shape the dough into a log about 12-inches long and 3 inches
   wide. Place it on the parchment paper-arranged baking sheet.
5. Bake for 23-25 minutes until golden brown. Remove and leave
   aside for 10 minutes.
6. Slice the log into ½-inch thick biscotti and lay the slices on the
   parchment paper-arranged baking sheet. Bake for another 10-15
   minutes until crisp.
7. Let the biscotti cool completely before serving.

**Prep Time:
20 mins**

**Cook Time:
45 mins**

**Serving
12 biscotti**

Salted Caramel Pecan Bars

Nutrition

Calories: 260 | Protein: 3g | Carbohydrate: 25g | Fat: 18g |
Fiber: 2g

Ingredients

For the crust:
1 ½ cups gluten-free all-purpose
flour
1 teaspoon xanthan gum
½ cup cold butter (or dairy-free
alternative), cubed
¼ cup coconut sugar
For the filling:
¾ cup coconut sugar
½ cup honey
¼ cup coconut oil (or butter)
2 cups chopped pecans
1 teaspoon vanilla extract
½ teaspoon sea salt (for sprinkling)

Instructions

1. Preheat oven to 350°F (175°C). Grease an 8x8-inch baking
   pan.
2. For the crust, combine the flour, xanthan gum, and coconut
   sugar. Cut in cold butter until it forms coarse crumbs. Press the
   mixture toward the bottom of the prepared pan.
3. Bake the crust for 10-12 minutes.
4. For the filling, in a saucepan over moderate flame, melt the
   coconut sugar, honey, and coconut oil until smooth. Toss in
   chopped pecans and vanilla extract.
5. Drop filling over the pre-baked crust and sprinkle with sea salt.
6. Bake for another 12-15 minutes until bubbling and golden.
7. Cool the bars before slicing into squares.

**Prep Time:
15 mins**

**Cook Time:
25 mins**

**Serving
12 bars**

Date and Walnut Bars

Nutrition

Calories: 220 | Protein: 3g | Carbohydrate: 33g | Fat: 10g | Fiber: 4g

Ingredients

1 cup gluten-free oats
1 ½ cups gluten-free all-purpose flour
1 teaspoon xanthan gum
½ cup melted coconut oil
½ cup coconut sugar
½ teaspoon baking soda
1 cup pitted dates, chopped
½ cup chopped walnuts
½ cup water

Instructions

1. Preheat oven to 350°F (175°C). Grease an 8x8-inch baking pan.
2. Grab the deep-bottom bowl and mix oats, flour, xanthan gum, coconut sugar, and baking soda. Toss in melted coconut oil until crumbly.
3. Press mixture (use half) toward the bottom of the prepared pan.
4. In a small pan, toss the chopped dates with water. Cook over medium heat, stirring until the dates break down and form a paste.
5. Spread the date mixture over the crust smoothly. Sprinkle chopped walnuts on top.
6. Crumble the leftover oat mixture over the date filling.
7. Bake for 20-25 minutes until golden brown. Leave it aside to cool before slicing.

Prep Time: 15 mins

Cook Time: 25 mins

Serving 12 bars

Pumpkin Cheesecake Bars

Nutrition

Calories: 200 | Protein: 4g | Carbohydrate: 26g | Fat: 9g | Fiber: 2g

Ingredients

For the crust:

1 ½ cups gluten-free graham cracker crumbs
¼ cup melted butter (or coconut oil)

For the filling:

8 oz dairy-free cream cheese
¾ cup coconut sugar
1 cup pumpkin puree
2 large eggs
1 teaspoon vanilla extract
1 teaspoon ground cinnamon
½ teaspoon ground ginger
¼ teaspoon ground cloves

Instructions

1. Preheat oven to 350°F (175°C). Grease an 8x8-inch baking pan.
2. For the crust, toss the graham cracker crumbs with melted butter. Press the mixture toward the bottom of the prepared pan.
3. For the filling, in a dee-bottom bowl, beat the dairy-free cream cheese and coconut sugar until smooth.
4. Add pumpkin puree, eggs, vanilla extract, cinnamon, ginger, and cloves. Mix until well combined.
5. Spread filling over the crust and smooth the top. Bake for 35-40 minutes until the center is set.
6. Leave it aside to cool completely before refrigerating for two hours (at least). Slice into bars before serving.

Prep Time:
20 mins

Cook Time:
40 mins

Serving
12 bars

S'mores Cookie Bars

Nutrition

Calories: 250 | Protein: 3g | Carbohydrate: 36g | Fat: 10g |
Fiber: 2g

Ingredients

1 ½ cups gluten-free graham
cracker crumbs
½ cup melted butter (or coconut
oil)
½ cup coconut sugar
1 ½ cups dairy-free chocolate chips
1 ½ cups mini marshmallows
(gluten-free)
1 cup gluten-free all-purpose flour
1 teaspoon xanthan gum
½ teaspoon baking soda
¼ teaspoon salt
1 large egg
1 teaspoon vanilla extract

Instructions

1. Preheat oven to 350°F (175°C). Grease an 8x8-inch baking
   pan.
2. Grab the deep-bottom bowl and combine the graham cracker
   crumbs, melted butter, and coconut sugar. Press the mixture
   toward the bottom of the prepared pan.
3. In another deep-bottom bowl, toss the flour with xanthan gum,
   baking soda, and salt.
4. Toss in the egg, vanilla extract, and a small portion of the
   marshmallows and chocolate chips into the flour mixture.
5. Spread this dough over the graham cracker crust. Top with
   leftover marshmallows and chocolate chips.
6. Bake for 23-25 minutes until marshmallows are slightly toasted.
7. Leave it aside to cool before slicing into bars.

**Prep Time:
15 mins**

**Cook Time:
25 mins**

**Serving
12 bars**

Pastries and Scones

Gooey Cinnamon Rolls with Icing

Nutrition

Calories: 240 | Protein: 3g | Carbohydrate: 38g | Fat: 9g |
Fiber: 2g

Ingredients

For the dough:
2 cups gluten-free all-purpose flour
1 teaspoon xanthan gum
1 packet (2 ¼ teaspoons) active dry
yeast
½ cup warm milk (or dairy-free
alternative)
¼ cup coconut sugar
¼ cup melted butter (or coconut oil)
1 large egg
1 teaspoon vanilla extract
For the filling:
¼ cup melted butter (or coconut oil)
½ cup coconut sugar
1 tablespoon ground cinnamon
For the icing:
1 cup powdered sugar (gluten-free)
2 tablespoons milk (or dairy-free
alternative)
½ teaspoon vanilla extract

Instructions

1. Take a small shallow bowl and mix warm milk, yeast, and
   one tbsp coconut sugar. Let sit for 5-10 minutes until frothy.
2. Take a deep-bottom bowl and combine the flour, xanthan gum,
   leftover coconut sugar, melted butter, egg, and vanilla extract.
   Add yeast mixture and toss until the dough forms.
3. Knead the dough for some minutes, then cover and put it aside
   to rise for 1 hour until doubled in size.
4. Roll the dough into a rectangle on the flour-dusted smooth
   surface. Spread melted butter in smooth way over the dough
   and sprinkle with the cinnamon and coconut sugar mixture.
5. Roll the dough tightly, then slice into 12 rolls. Place the rolls and
   let them rise for 30 minutes.
6. Preheat oven to 350°F (175°C). Bake the rolls for 22-25 minutes.
7. For the icing, toss the powdered sugar, milk, and vanilla extract.
   Drizzle over the warm rolls before serving.

**Prep Time:
20 mins**

**Cook Time:
25 mins**

**Serving
12 rolls**

CRANBERRY ORANGE SCONES

Nutrition

Calories: 220 | Protein: 4g | Carbohydrate: 32g | Fat: 9g |
Fiber: 2g

Ingredients

2 cups gluten-free all-purpose flour
1 teaspoon xanthan gum
1 tablespoon baking powder
¼ cup coconut sugar
½ teaspoon salt
½ cup cold butter (or coconut oil)
1 large egg
½ cup milk (or dairy-free alternative)
1 tablespoon orange zest
½ cup dried cranberries

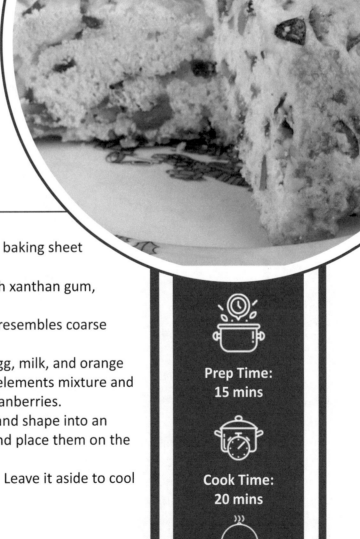

Instructions

1. Preheat oven to 400°F (200°C). Arrange the baking sheet
   with parchment paper.
2. Take a deep-bottom bowl and mix flour with xanthan gum,
   baking powder, coconut sugar, and salt.
3. Toss in cold butter pieces until the mixture resembles coarse
   crumbs.
4. Take the other shallow bowl and toss the egg, milk, and orange
   zest. Add wet elements mixture to the dry elements mixture and
   stir until just combined. Fold in the dried cranberries.
5. Turn the dough out onto a floured surface and shape into an
   8-inch circle. Cut the circle into 8 wedges and place them on the
   parchment paper-arranged baking sheet.
6. Bake for 18-20 minutes until golden brown. Leave it aside to cool
   before serving.

Prep Time:
15 mins

Cook Time:
20 mins

Serving
8 scones

Flaky Cheese Danish

Nutrition

Calories: 290 | Protein: 4g | Carbohydrate: 40g | Fat: 14g | Fiber: 2g

Ingredients

For the dough:

2 ½ cups gluten-free all-purpose flour

1 teaspoon xanthan gum

1 tablespoon sugar

½ teaspoon salt

1 cup cold butter (or coconut oil), cubed

½ cup cold water

For the filling:

8 oz dairy-free cream cheese

¼ cup coconut sugar

1 teaspoon vanilla extract

For the glaze:

1 cup powdered sugar

2 tablespoons milk (or dairy-free alternative)

½ teaspoon vanilla extract

Instructions

1. Take a deep-bottom bowl and mix flour, xanthan gum, sugar, and salt. Toss in cold butter pieces until the mixture resembles coarse crumbs. Gradually add chill water and mix until a dough forms.
2. Wrap the dough and leave to chill for 30 minutes.
3. For the filling, beat together the dairy-free cream cheese, coconut sugar, and vanilla extract until smooth.
4. Preheat oven to 400°F (200°C). Roll out the dough on the flour-dusted smooth surface and cut into 8 rectangles.
5. Place a spoonful of filling in the center of each rectangle and fold the edges over. Bake for 18-20 minutes until golden brown.
6. For the glaze, toss the powdered sugar, milk, and vanilla extract. Drizzle over the cooled danishes before serving.

**Prep Time:
20 mins**

**Cook Time:
20 mins**

**Serving
8 danishes**

Puff Pastry with Apple Filling

Nutrition

Calories: 280 | Protein: 3g | Carbohydrate: 40g | Fat: 14g |
Fiber: 3g

Ingredients

For the pastry:
2 ½ cups gluten-free all-purpose
flour
1 teaspoon xanthan gum
1 tablespoon sugar
½ teaspoon salt
1 cup cold butter (or coconut oil),
cubed
½ cup cold water
For the filling:
3 large apples, peeled and chopped
¼ cup coconut sugar
1 teaspoon ground cinnamon
1 tablespoon cornstarch

Instructions

1. Take a deep-bottom bowl and mix flour, xanthan gum,
   sugar, and salt. Cut in cold butter until the mixture forms coarse
   crumbs. Gradually add chill water (add water in small portions)
   and mix until a dough forms.
2. Wrap the dough and leave to chill for 30 minutes.
3. For the filling, combine the chopped apples with coconut sugar,
   cinnamon, and cornstarch in a saucepan. Cook over moderate
   flame until the apples soften, and the mixture thickens. Leave it
   aside to cool.
4. Preheat oven to 400°F (200°C). Roll out the dough on the flour-
   dusted smooth surface and cut into 8 rectangles. Spoon the
   apple filling into the center of each rectangle and fold the edges
   over.
5. Bake for 18-20 minutes until golden brown. Leave it aside to cool
   before serving.

**Prep Time:
20 mins**

**Cook Time:
20 mins**

**Serving
8 pastries**

Sweet Peach Turnovers

Nutrition

Calories: 270 | Protein: 3g | Carbohydrate: 38g | Fat: 13g | Fiber: 2g

Ingredients

For the pastry:
2 ½ cups gluten-free all-purpose flour
1 teaspoon xanthan gum
1 tablespoon sugar
½ teaspoon salt
1 cup cold butter (or coconut oil), cubed
½ cup cold water
For the filling:
3 large peaches, peeled and chopped
¼ cup coconut sugar
1 teaspoon ground cinnamon
1 tablespoon cornstarch

Instructions

1. Take a deep-bottom bowl and mix flour, xanthan gum, sugar, and salt. Cut in cold butter until the mixture forms coarse crumbs. Add chill water and mix until a dough forms.
2. Wrap the dough and chill for 30 minutes.
3. For the filling, combine chopped peaches, coconut sugar, cinnamon, and cornstarch in a saucepan. Cook over moderate flame until the peaches soften, and the mixture thickens. Leave it aside to cool.
4. Preheat oven to 400°F (200°C). Roll out the dough on the flour-dusted smooth surface and cut into 8 rectangles. Spoon the peach filling into the center of each rectangle and fold the edges over.
5. Bake for 18-20 minutes until golden brown. Leave it aside to cool before serving.

**Prep Time:
20 mins**

**Cook Time:
20 mins**

**Serving
8 turnovers**

Chocolate-Filled Croissants

Nutrition

Calories: 320 | Protein: 5g | Carbohydrate: 36g | Fat: 18g |
Fiber: 2g

Ingredients

For the dough:
2 ½ cups gluten-free all-purpose
flour
1 teaspoon xanthan gum
2 teaspoons active dry yeast
½ cup warm milk (or dairy-free
alternative)
¼ cup coconut sugar
1 cup cold butter (or dairy-free
alternative), cubed
2 large eggs
1 teaspoon vanilla extract
For the filling:
1 cup dairy-free chocolate chips

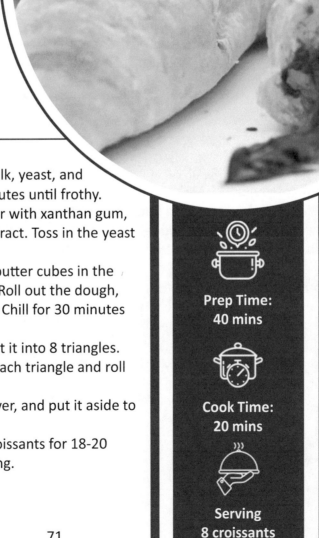

Instructions

1. Take a small shallow bowl and mix warm milk, yeast, and
   one tbsp coconut sugar. Let sit for 5-10 minutes until frothy.
2. Take a deep-bottom bowl and combine flour with xanthan gum,
   leftover coconut sugar, eggs, and vanilla extract. Toss in the yeast
   mixture until a dough forms.
3. Roll the dough into a rectangle, place cold butter cubes in the
   center, and fold the dough over the butter. Roll out the dough,
   fold it into thirds, and repeat 2 more times. Chill for 30 minutes
   between folds.
4. Roll the dough into a large rectangle and cut it into 8 triangles.
   Place a few chocolate chips at the base of each triangle and roll
   it up into a croissant shape.
5. Place the croissants on a greased sheet, cover, and put it aside to
   rise for 1 hour.
6. Preheat oven to 375°F (190°C). Bake the croissants for 18-20
   minutes. Leave it aside to cool before serving.

Prep Time:
40 mins

Cook Time:
20 mins

Serving
8 croissants

Blueberry Lemon Scones

Nutrition

Calories: 230 | Protein: 4g | Carbohydrate: 33g | Fat: 9g |
Fiber: 3g

Ingredients

2 cups gluten-free all-purpose flour
1 teaspoon xanthan gum
1 tablespoon baking powder
¼ cup coconut sugar
½ teaspoon salt
½ cup cold butter (or coconut oil)
1 large egg
½ cup milk (or dairy-free
alternative)
1 tablespoon lemon zest
1 cup fresh or frozen blueberries

Instructions

1. Preheat oven to 400°F (200°C). Arrange the baking sheet
    with parchment paper.
2. Take a deep-bottom bowl and mix flour with xanthan gum,
    baking powder, coconut sugar, and salt.
3. Toss in cold butter pieces until the mixture resembles coarse
    crumbs.
4. Take the other shallow bowl and toss the egg, milk, and lemon
    zest. Add wet elements mixture to the dry elements mixture and
    stir until just combined. Fold in the blueberries.
5. Turn the dough out onto a floured surface and shape into an
    8-inch circle. Cut the circle into 8 wedges and place them on the
    parchment paper-arranged baking sheet.
6. Bake for 18-20 minutes until golden brown. Leave it aside to cool
    before serving.

Prep Time:
15 mins

Cook Time:
20 mins

Serving
8 scones

Savory Cheddar and Chive Scones

Nutrition

Calories: 250 | Protein: 7g | Carbohydrate: 30g | Fat: 12g | Fiber: 2g

Ingredients

2 cups gluten-free all-purpose flour
1 teaspoon xanthan gum
1 tablespoon baking powder
½ teaspoon salt
½ cup cold butter (or coconut oil)
1 large egg
½ cup milk (or dairy-free alternative)
1 cup shredded cheddar cheese (dairy-free, if needed)
2 tablespoons chopped fresh chives

Instructions

1. Preheat oven to 400°F (200°C). Arrange the baking sheet with parchment paper.
2. Take a deep-bottom bowl and mix flour with xanthan gum, baking powder, and salt.
3. Toss in cold butter pieces until the mixture resembles coarse crumbs.
4. Take the other shallow bowl and toss the egg and milk. Add wet elements mixture to the dry elements mixture and stir until just combined. Fold in the cheddar cheese and chives.
5. Turn the dough out onto a floured surface and shape into an 8-inch circle. Cut the circle into 8 wedges and place them on the parchment paper-arranged baking sheet.
6. Bake for 18-20 minutes until golden brown. Leave it aside to cool before serving.

Prep Time:
15 mins

Cook Time:
20 mins

Serving
8 scones

Lemon Curd Danish with Pastry Crust

Nutrition

Calories: 290 | Protein: 3g | Carbohydrate: 40g | Fat: 14g | Fiber: 2g

Ingredients

For the pastry:
2 ½ cups gluten-free all-purpose flour
1 teaspoon xanthan gum
1 tablespoon sugar
½ teaspoon salt
1 cup cold butter (or coconut oil), cubed
½ cup cold water
For the filling:
½ cup lemon curd (store-bought or homemade)
For the glaze:
1 cup powdered sugar
2 tablespoons milk (or dairy-free alternative)
½ teaspoon vanilla extract

Instructions

1. Take a deep-bottom bowl and mix flour, xanthan gum, sugar, and salt. Toss in cold butter pieces until the mixture resembles coarse crumbs. Add chill water and mix until a dough forms.
2. Wrap the dough and chill for 30 minutes.
3. Preheat oven to 400°F (200°C). Roll out the dough on the flour-dusted smooth surface and cut into 8 rectangles.
4. Place a spoonful of lemon curd in the center of each rectangle and fold the edges over.
5. Bake for 18-20 minutes until golden brown.
6. For the glaze, toss the powdered sugar, milk, and vanilla extract. Drizzle over the cooled danishes before serving.

Prep Time:
20 mins

Cook Time:
20 mins

Serving
8 danishes

Classic Eclairs with Vanilla Filling

Nutrition

Calories: 230 | Protein: 4g | Carbohydrate: 30g | Fat: 11g | Fiber: 1g

Ingredients

For the pastry:
1 cup gluten-free all-purpose flour
1 teaspoon xanthan gum
½ cup butter (or coconut oil)
1 cup water
4 large eggs
For the filling:
1 cup dairy-free vanilla pudding
(store-bought or homemade)
For the chocolate glaze:
½ cup dairy-free chocolate chips
¼ cup coconut milk

Instructions

1. Preheat oven to 400°F (200°C). Arrange the baking sheet with parchment paper.
2. In a saucepan, get water and butter to a boil. Remove from heat and toss in flour and xanthan gum (if needed) until the dough forms a ball.
3. Beat in the eggs, one at a time, until the dough looks smooth and glossy.
4. Fill the dough into the piping bag and pipe 4-inch strips onto the parchment paper-arranged baking sheet.
5. Bake for 20-25 minutes. Leave it aside to cool.
6. For the filling, spoon the vanilla pudding into a piping bag and fill the cooled eclairs.
7. For the glaze, melt the chocolate chips with coconut milk. Dip the eclairs top into the chocolate glaze before serving.

Prep Time:
30 mins

Cook Time:
25 mins

Serving
12 eclairs

Profiteroles with Chocolate Glaze

Nutrition

Calories: 180 | Protein: 3g | Carbohydrate: 20g | Fat: 10g | Fiber: 1g

Ingredients

For the pastry:
1 cup gluten-free all-purpose flour
1 teaspoon xanthan gum
½ cup butter (or coconut oil)
1 cup water
4 large eggs

For the filling:
1 cup dairy-free whipped cream or vanilla ice cream

For the chocolate glaze:
½ cup dairy-free chocolate chips
¼ cup coconut milk

Instructions

1. Preheat oven to 400°F (200°C). Arrange the baking sheet with parchment paper.
2. In a saucepan, get it water and butter to a boil. Remove from heat and toss in flour and xanthan gum (if needed) until the dough forms a ball.
3. Beat in the eggs, one at a time, until the dough looks smooth and glossy.
4. Ladle dough into the piping bag and pipe small mounds onto the prepared baking sheet.
5. Bake for 22-25 minutes until puffed. Leave it aside to cool.
6. Slice the profiteroles in half and fill them with whipped cream or vanilla ice cream.
7. For the glaze, melt the chocolate chips with coconut milk until smooth. Drizzle over the filled profiteroles before serving.

**Prep Time:
25 mins**

**Cook Time:
25 mins**

**Serving
12 profiteroles**

Strawberry and Cream Scones

Nutrition

Calories: 220 | Protein: 4g | Carbohydrate: 32g | Fat: 9g |
Fiber: 2g

Ingredients

2 cups gluten-free all-purpose flour
1 teaspoon xanthan gum
1 tablespoon baking powder
¼ cup coconut sugar
½ teaspoon salt
½ cup cold butter (or coconut oil)
1 large egg
½ cup milk (or dairy-free
alternative)
1 cup fresh strawberries, chopped
½ cup dairy-free whipped cream
(for topping)

Instructions

1. Preheat oven to 400°F (200°C). Arrange the baking sheet
   with parchment paper.
2. Take a deep-bottom bowl and mix flour with xanthan gum,
   baking powder, coconut sugar, and salt.
3. Toss in cold butter pieces until the mixture resembles coarse
   crumbs.
4. Take the other shallow bowl and toss the egg and milk. Add wet
   elements mixture to the dry elements mixture and stir until just
   combined. Fold in the chopped strawberries.
5. Turn the dough out onto a floured surface and shape into an
   8-inch circle. Cut the circle into 8 wedges and place them on the
   parchment paper-arranged baking sheet.
6. Bake for 18-20 minutes until golden brown. Leave it aside to cool
   slightly, then top with whipped cream before serving.

Prep Time:
15 mins

Cook Time:
20 mins

Serving
8 scones

Almond Croissants with Marzipan

Nutrition

Calories: 310 | Protein: 6g | Carbohydrate: 34g | Fat: 18g |
Fiber: 2g

Ingredients

For the dough:
2 ½ cups gluten-free all-purpose
flour
1 teaspoon xanthan gum
2 teaspoons active dry yeast
½ cup warm milk (or dairy-free
alternative)
¼ cup coconut sugar
1 cup cold butter (or dairy-free
alternative), cubed
2 large eggs
1 teaspoon vanilla extract
For the filling:
½ cup marzipan, softened
¼ cup almond flour
For topping:
¼ cup sliced almonds

Instructions

1. Take a small shallow bowl and mix warm milk, yeast, and
   one tbsp coconut sugar. Let sit for 5-10 minutes until frothy.
2. Take a deep-bottom bowl and combine flour with xanthan gum,
   leftover coconut sugar, eggs, and vanilla extract. Toss in the yeast
   mixture until a dough forms.
3. Roll the dough into a rectangle, place cold butter cubes in the
   center, and fold the dough over the butter. Roll out the dough,
   fold it into thirds, and repeat 2 more times. Chill for 30 minutes
   between folds.
4. Roll the dough into a large rectangle and cut it into 8 triangles.
   Spread a small amount of marzipan and almond flour mixture
   onto each triangle, then roll into croissant shapes.
5. Place the croissants on the greased sheet, cover, and let rise for
   1 hour.
6. Preheat oven to 375°F (190°C). Brush the tops with egg wash and
   spread with sliced almonds. Bake for 18-20 minutes until golden
   brown.

**Prep Time:
40 mins**

**Cook Time:
20 mins**

**Serving
12 8 croissants**

Peach and Almond Hand Pies

Nutrition

Calories: 280 | Protein: 4g | Carbohydrate: 38g | Fat: 13g |
Fiber: 3g

Ingredients

For the pastry:
2 ½ cups gluten-free all-purpose
flour
1 teaspoon xanthan gum
½ cup cold butter (or coconut oil)
1 tablespoon coconut sugar
½ teaspoon salt
½ cup cold water
For the filling:
3 ripe peaches, peeled and
chopped
¼ cup coconut sugar
1 tablespoon cornstarch
½ teaspoon almond extract
¼ cup sliced almonds (for topping)

Instructions

1. Preheat oven to 375°F (190°C). Arrange the baking sheet
   with parchment paper.
2. Take a deep-bottom bowl and mix flour, xanthan gum, sugar, and
   salt. Cut in cold butter until the mixture forms coarse crumbs.
   Add cold water in small portiuons and mix until a dough forms.
3. Roll out the dough on the flour-dusted smooth surface and cut
   into 8 circles.
4. Take a small shallow bowl and mix the chopped peaches,
   coconut sugar, cornstarch, and almond extract. Spread a portion
   of the filling onto one side of each dough circle and fold over.
   Crimp the edges to seal using the fork.
5. Place the hand pies on the parchment paper-arranged baking
   sheet and brush the top surface with some water. Sprinkle sliced
   almonds on top.
6. Bake for 20-25 minutes until golden brown. Leave it aside to cool
   before serving.

Prep Time:
20 mins

Cook Time:
25 mins

Serving
8 hand pies

Chocolate-Dipped Scones with Hazelnuts

Nutrition

Calories: 260 | Protein: 5g | Carbohydrate: 30g | Fat: 14g | Fiber: 3g

Ingredients

2 cups gluten-free all-purpose flour
1 teaspoon xanthan gum
1 tablespoon baking powder
¼ cup coconut sugar
½ teaspoon salt
½ cup cold butter (or coconut oil)
1 large egg
½ cup milk (or dairy-free alternative)
½ cup chopped hazelnuts
½ cup dairy-free chocolate chips

Instructions

1. Preheat oven to 400°F (200°C). Arrange the baking sheet with parchment paper.
2. Take a deep-bottom bowl and mix flour with xanthan gum, baking powder, coconut sugar, and salt.
3. Toss in cold butter pieces until the mixture resembles coarse crumbs.
4. Take the other shallow bowl and toss the egg and milk. Add wet elements mixture to the dry elements mixture and stir until just combined. Fold in the chopped hazelnuts.
5. Turn the dough out onto a floured surface and shape into an 8-inch circle. Cut the circle into 8 wedges and place them on the parchment paper-arranged baking sheet.
6. Bake for 18-20 minutes until golden brown. Leave it aside to cool completely.
7. Melt the chocolate chips by using another one method (microwave or double boiler). Dip one side of each scone into the melted chocolate and let it set before serving.

Prep Time: 15 mins

Cook Time: 20 mins

Serving 8 scones

Specialty and Holiday Bakes

Spiced Hot Cross Buns

Nutrition

Calories: 200 | Protein: 4g | Carbohydrate: 30g | Fat: 7g | Fiber: 2g

Ingredients

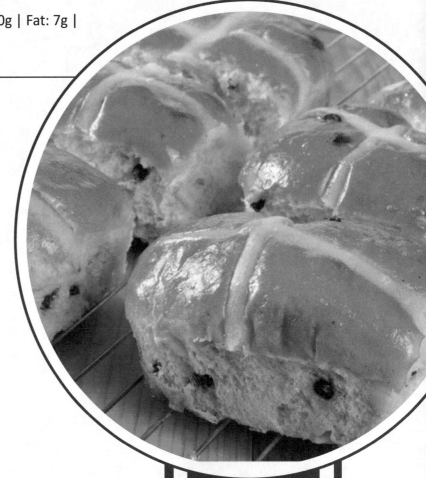

2 cups gluten-free all-purpose flour
1 teaspoon xanthan gum
1 packet (2 ¼ teaspoons) active dry yeast
½ cup warm milk (or dairy-free alternative)
¼ cup coconut sugar
1 teaspoon ground cinnamon
½ teaspoon ground nutmeg
½ teaspoon allspice
¼ teaspoon ground cloves
½ teaspoon salt
2 large eggs
¼ cup melted butter (or coconut oil)
½ cup dried currants or raisins
For the icing cross:
½ cup powdered sugar
1 tablespoon milk (or dairy-free alternative)

Instructions

1. Take a small shallow bowl and mix warm milk, yeast, and one tbsp coconut sugar. Let sit for 5-10 minutes until frothy.
2. Take a deep-bottom bowl and toss the flour with xanthan gum, leftover coconut sugar, cinnamon, nutmeg, allspice, cloves, and salt.
3. Add yeast mixture, eggs, melted butter, and currants. Mix until a dough forms.
4. Shape and divide the dough into 12 balls and place them in a greased baking dish. Cover and put them aside for 1 hour until doubled in size.
5. Preheat oven to 375°F (190°C). Bake the buns for 23-25 minutes. Leave it aside to cool slightly.
6. For the icing, toss the powdered sugar and milk. Pipe a cross on top of each bun before serving.

Prep Time:
20 mins

Cook Time:
25 mins

Serving
12 buns

Rich Fruitcake with Brandy

Nutrition

Calories: 290 | Protein: 4g | Carbohydrate: 35g | Fat: 14g | Fiber: 3g

Ingredients

1 ½ cups gluten-free all-purpose flour
1 teaspoon xanthan gum
1 teaspoon baking powder
½ teaspoon ground cinnamon
½ teaspoon ground nutmeg
½ teaspoon ground cloves
½ teaspoon salt
½ cup melted butter (or coconut oil)
¾ cup coconut sugar
3 large eggs
1 teaspoon vanilla extract
1 cup mixed dried fruits (raisins, currants, cranberries)
½ cup chopped nuts (walnuts, pecans)
¼ cup brandy (plus extra for brushing)

Instructions

1. Preheat oven to 325°F (160°C). Grease a loaf pan and arrange it with parchment paper.
2. Take a deep-bottom bowl and toss the flour, xanthan gum (if needed), baking powder, cinnamon, nutmeg, cloves, and salt.
3. Take the other shallow bowl and beat together melted butter, coconut sugar, eggs, and vanilla extract. Add wet elements mixture to the dry elements mixture and mix until smooth.
4. Fold in the dried fruits, chopped nuts, and brandy. Ladle batter into the oil-greased pan and smooth the top.
5. Bake for 1:30 hours until a tooth-stick is inserted and comes out clean. Leave it aside to cool slightly.
6. Brush the warm cake with extra brandy for added moisture. Put it aside to cool completely before slicing.

Prep Time:
30 mins

Cook Time:
1.30 hours

Serving
12 slices

German Stollen with Dried Fruits

Nutrition

Calories: 240 | Protein: 4g | Carbohydrate: 32g | Fat: 10g | Fiber: 2g

Ingredients

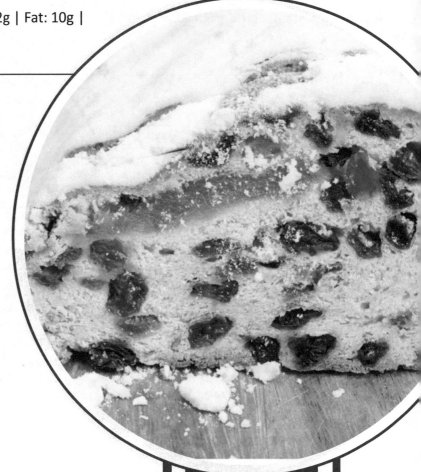

2 ½ cups gluten-free all-purpose flour
1 teaspoon xanthan gum
1 packet (2 ¼ teaspoons) active dry yeast
½ cup warm milk (or dairy-free alternative)
¼ cup coconut sugar
½ teaspoon salt
½ teaspoon ground cinnamon
¼ teaspoon ground nutmeg
¼ teaspoon ground cardamom
1 large egg
¼ cup melted butter (or coconut oil)
½ cup dried fruits (raisins, currants, chopped apricots)
¼ cup chopped almonds
1 teaspoon vanilla extract
For dusting:
½ cup powdered sugar

Instructions

1. Take a small shallow bowl and mix warm milk, yeast, and one tbsp coconut sugar. Let sit for 5-10 minutes until frothy.
2. Take a deep-bottom bowl and toss the flour with xanthan gum, leftover coconut sugar, salt, cinnamon, nutmeg, and cardamom.
3. Add yeast mixture, egg, melted butter, dried fruits, almonds, and vanilla extract. Mix until a dough forms.
4. Shape the dough into a log and place it on a greased baking sheet. Cover and let rise for 1 hour.
5. Preheat oven to 350°F (175°C). Bake for 37-40 minutes until golden brown. Leave it aside to cool slightly.
6. Dust the stollen generously with powdered sugar before slicing and serving.

**Prep Time:
30 mins**

**Cook Time:
40 mins**

**Serving
12 slices**

Italian Panettone with Raisins

Nutrition

Calories: 250 | Protein: 5g | Carbohydrate: 35g | Fat: 10g |
Fiber: 2g

Ingredients

2 ½ cups gluten-free all-purpose
flour
1 teaspoon xanthan gum
1 packet (2 ¼ teaspoons) active dry
yeast
½ cup warm milk (or dairy-free
alternative)
¼ cup coconut sugar
½ teaspoon salt
1 teaspoon vanilla extract
½ teaspoon ground cinnamon
¼ teaspoon ground nutmeg
3 large eggs
½ cup melted butter (or coconut
oil)
½ cup raisins
¼ cup chopped candied orange peel

Instructions

1. Take a small shallow bowl and mix warm milk, yeast, and
   one tbsp coconut sugar. Let sit for 5-10 minutes until frothy.
2. Take a deep-bottom bowl and toss the flour with xanthan gum,
   leftover coconut sugar, salt, cinnamon, and nutmeg.
3. Add yeast mixture, vanilla extract, eggs, melted butter, raisins,
   and candied orange peel. Mix until a smooth dough forms.
4. Place the dough in a greased round panettone mold or a deep
   round cake pan. Cover and put it aside for one hour until
   doubled in size.
5. Preheat oven to 350°F (175°C). Bake for 35-40 minutes until
   golden brown.
6. Leave it aside to cool before slicing and serving.

**Prep Time:
30 mins**

**Cook Time:
40 mins**

**Serving
12 slices**

Traditional Christmas Pudding

Nutrition

Calories: 320 | Protein: 4g | Carbohydrate: 45g | Fat: 14g |
Fiber: 3g

Ingredients

1 ½ cups gluten-free breadcrumbs
½ cup coconut sugar
1 teaspoon ground cinnamon
½ teaspoon ground nutmeg
½ teaspoon ground cloves
1 cup mixed dried fruits (raisins,
currants, chopped dates)
½ cup chopped nuts (walnuts,
almonds)
¼ cup brandy
2 large eggs
½ cup melted butter (or coconut
oil)
¼ cup milk (or dairy-free
alternative)

Instructions

1. Take a deep-bottom bowl and mix breadcrumbs with
   coconut sugar, cinnamon, nutmeg, cloves, dried fruits, and nuts.
2. Take the other shallow bowl and toss the brandy, eggs, melted
   butter, and milk. Add wet elements mixture to the dry mixture
   and stir until combined.
3. Ladle mixture into the pudding basin or mold and cover tightly
   with foil.
4. Place the pudding mixture in a large pot and fill the pot halfway
   with water. Bring to a simmer and steam for 3 hours, checking
   the water level periodically.
5. Remove the pudding from the pot and leave aside to cool slightly
   before unmolding.
6. Serve warm, optionally with brandy butter or custard.

**Prep Time:
30 mins**

**Cook Time:
3 hours**

**Serving
8**

Pumpkin Spice Bread Pudding

Nutrition

Calories: 240 | Protein: 6g | Carbohydrate: 35g | Fat: 8g |
Fiber: 2g

Ingredients

4 cups gluten-free bread cubes
1 cup pumpkin puree
¾ cup coconut sugar
2 large eggs
1 teaspoon vanilla extract
1 teaspoon ground cinnamon
½ teaspoon ground nutmeg
½ teaspoon ground ginger
2 cups milk (or dairy-free alternative)

Instructions

1. Preheat oven to 350°F (175°C). Grease a baking dish.
2. Take a deep-bottom bowl and toss the pumpkin puree, coconut sugar, eggs, vanilla, cinnamon, nutmeg, ginger, and milk.
3. Add gluten-free bread cubes to the mixture and stir to coat evenly. Let the bread soak for 10 minutes.
4. Ladle mixture into the greased baking dish and bake for 35-40 minutes or until set and golden brown.
5. Serve warm, optionally, with maple syrup or whipped cream.

Prep Time:
15 mins

Cook Time:
40 mins

Serving
8

Yule Log Cake with Chocolate Frosting

Nutrition

Calories: 260 | Protein: 4g | Carbohydrate: 35g | Fat: 12g |
Fiber: 2g

Ingredients

For the cake:
1 cup gluten-free all-purpose flour
1 teaspoon xanthan gum
¼ cup cocoa powder
1 teaspoon baking powder
¼ teaspoon salt
¾ cup coconut sugar
4 large eggs
1 teaspoon vanilla extract
For the filling:
1 cup dairy-free whipped cream
For the chocolate frosting:
1 cup dairy-free chocolate chips
½ cup coconut milk

Instructions

1. Preheat oven to 350°F (175°C). Grease a roll pan and arrange it with parchment paper.
2. Grab the deep-bottom bowl and toss the flour, xanthan gum (if needed), cocoa powder, baking powder, and salt.
3. In another deep-bottom bowl, beat the eggs, coconut sugar, and vanilla extract. Toss in dry ingredients in small portions into the egg mixture until smooth.
4. Spread the batter evenly onto the greased pan. Bake for 12-15 minutes until the cake springs back when touched.
5. While the cake is still warm, carefully roll it up on the parchment paper and let it cool completely.
6. For the filling, spread whipped cream over the unrolled cake and roll it back up.
7. For the frosting, melt the chocolate chips with coconut milk until smooth. Spread the frosting over the cake roll. Let it set before serving.

Prep Time:
30 mins

Cook Time:
15 mins

Serving
12 slices

Easter Braided Sweet Bread

Nutrition

Calories: 230 | Protein: 5g | Carbohydrate: 33g | Fat: 8g |
Fiber: 2g

Ingredients

2 ½ cups gluten-free all-purpose
flour
1 teaspoon xanthan gum
1 packet (2 ¼ teaspoons) active dry
yeast
½ cup warm milk (or dairy-free
alternative)
¼ cup coconut sugar
½ teaspoon salt
1 teaspoon vanilla extract
½ teaspoon ground cinnamon
¼ teaspoon ground nutmeg
3 large eggs
¼ cup melted butter (or coconut oil)

Instructions

1. Take a small shallow bowl and mix warm milk, yeast, and
   one tbsp coconut sugar. Let sit for 5-10 minutes until frothy.
2. Take a deep-bottom bowl and toss the flour with xanthan gum,
   leftover coconut sugar, salt, cinnamon, and nutmeg.
3. Add yeast mixture, vanilla extract, 2 eggs, and melted butter. Mix
   until a smooth dough forms.
4. Divide the dough evenly into 3 segments and roll each portion
   into a long rope. Braid the ropes together and place the braided
   dough on a greased baking sheet.
5. Cover and let rise for 1 hour.
6. Preheat oven to 350°F (175°C). Brush the braided dough with
   the remaining egg (beaten). Bake for 20-25 minutes until golden
   brown.
7. Leave it aside to cool before slicing.

**Prep Time:
30 mins**

**Cook Time:
25 mins**

**Serving
12 slices**

Cranberry and Orange Holiday Bread

Nutrition

Calories: 190 | Protein: 3g | Carbohydrate: 28g | Fat: 7g | Fiber: 2gv

Ingredients

1 ½ cups gluten-free all-purpose flour
1 teaspoon xanthan gum
1 teaspoon baking powder
½ teaspoon baking soda
½ teaspoon salt
½ cup coconut sugar
¼ cup melted coconut oil
1 large egg
½ cup orange juice
1 tablespoon orange zest
1 cup fresh or frozen cranberries

Instructions

1. Preheat oven to 350°F (175°C). Grease a loaf pan.
2. Grab the deep-bottom bowl and toss the flour with xanthan gum, baking powder, baking soda, salt, and coconut sugar.
3. In another deep-bottom bowl, toss the melted coconut oil with egg, orange juice, and orange zest. Gradually add dry elements mixture to the wet elements mixture and mix until just combined. Fold in the cranberries.
4. Pour the batter into the oil greased pan and bake for 35-40 minutes, or until a tooth-stick is inserted and comes out clean.
5. Cool the bread for 8-10 minutes.

Prep Time: 15 mins

Cook Time: 40 mins

Serving 12 slices

Conclusion

Thank you for joining us on this gluten-free baking journey through the seasons! The Ultimate Gluten-Free Holiday Cookbook was created to inspire joyful, flavorful, and inclusive celebrations, making it possible for everyone at the table to enjoy the holiday magic of baking—gluten-free and full of love.

As you've explored these recipes, from indulgent Yule log cakes to fragrant spiced breads, you've uncovered new ways to bring classic holiday flavors to life without compromising taste or tradition. Each recipe was crafted to make baking fun, straightforward, and accessible, allowing you to create delightful treats that look and taste just like the memories you cherish.

Baking for the holidays is more than just making desserts; it's a way to gather, share, and celebrate with the people we love most. We hope this cookbook has given you the tools and inspiration to make every holiday a little brighter and more delicious. May these gluten-free treats fill your home with warmth, joy, and the magic of each season.

Thank you for letting us be part of your holiday celebrations. Here's to many more years of festive baking, sharing, and savoring—all gluten-free and from the heart. Happy holidays!

27201899R00051